TO MARKET TO MARKET

AN
OLD-FASHIONED
FAMILY STORY:
THE
WEST SIDE MARKET

By JOANNE M. LEWIS

DESIGN AND PHOTOGRAPHY
By JOHN SZILAGYI

Editor: Suzanne Ringler Jones

With a forward by
Congresswoman Mary Rose Oakar

Elandon Books, Inc.,
Cleveland Heights, Ohio : 1981

To Robert
my best friend, my husband, who held my hand and
guided me through the scholarship and the sauerkraut.
J. M. L.

To Market/To Market

Copyright 1981 by Elandon Books, Inc.

first printing

designed by John Szilagyi, has been set in Cheltenham and printed by Carpenter
Reserve Printing Company in an edition of 10,000 copies, of which 9,000 are
bound in soft covers. Of the 1,000 copies bound in hard covers, 100 are reserved
for a special deluxe edition.

© 1981 by Elandon Books, Inc.
2115 Elandon Dr., Cleveland Heights, Ohio 44106

Distributed by Edgewater Book Co., Inc.
P.O. Box 586, Lakewood, Ohio 44107

Library of Congress Catalog Card No: 81-70026

Soft Cover   ISBN   0-937424-11-0
Hard Cover   ISBN   0-937424-12-9

CONTENTS

Among my earliest memories as a child, I remember walking with my father from our home on West 30th Street to the West Side Market. It was always there! We carried two shopping bags, knowing we would fill at least six. I thought my dad was the strongest man in the world because he always managed all of them.

The products were beautiful and as colorful as the people. The hues and colors of the fruits and vegetables, the mellow aromas of the bakeries, the freshness of the meats and fish. To me the West Side Market manifested adventure — an adventure in sights, sounds, colors, aromas — an adventure in seeing and knowing people — an adventure in taste, friendship and love. My father knew everyone, and the marketeers called him "Joe."

They wanted him to have the best for his family — for his wife and their five children. Times were not easy. World War II was still raging, but the merchants saved their best for us — a few more ounces of meat, a shiny apple, more salted butter, fresh eggs and raw vegetables.

The West Side Market is my legacy. I have always known the grandparents, parents and children — the generations of people who run the stands — the Tricskos, the Ehrnfelts, the Webers, the Simmelinks, the Ralofskys, the Peters, the Leus, the Coynes, the Rinis, to name a few. They are all part of my youth and adulthood.

Today our Market is more vital than ever. The diverse ethnicity of the people — a microcosm not only of Cleveland, but also of the World.

The West Side Market satisfies our human needs for food. It provides human contact for friends, neighbors, merchants, and it fulfills the need for public servants to be at their best, to meet and listen to the grassroots people. It is the place Clevelanders show off to new friends.

A consumer's delight, specialties which everyone can afford, a politician's dream crowd, the hub of the area, the life center of Cleveland.

The West Side Market is the heartbeat of Cleveland — our life's blood which sustains us. I still live on West 30th Street and walk down to the Market. It is still an adventure for me. It is still so cherished — so much a part of my past — so much a part of my future. Fortunately, nothing has changed. It is as wonderful and as alive as ever. It will continue to grow with future generations providing for each other in much the same simple, lovely way. No other place in the world is like it, and it belongs to all of us, no matter how rich, how poor, how young, how old, how white, how black. It signals optimism and hope — a living legacy for us all! It is truly one of life's finest pleasures.

Mary Rose Oakar

Member of Congress
20th District, Ohio

To market, to market,
to buy a fat pig,
Home again, home again,
jiggety-jig;
To market, to market,
to buy a fat hog,
Home again, home again,
jiggety jog.

More than 400 years ago this small nursery rhyme was inscribed in a dictionary of verse, and it has been known in one form or another ever since. Long before it was finally written down, generations of mothers surely sat their babies on their knees, bouncing and reciting the eternal verse: Home-Market; Market-Home. Whatever the Market is called, this meeting place where people gather to buy, to sell, to be together, has always been at the hub of society as we know it. Every child has learned that.

To buy a fat pig. To hear news, to carry on business, to engage in politics, to be entertained, to meet a friend or stranger — people come "To Market." The mother, adjusting her basket over her arm, taking her child by the hand, leading the way to the market place — to witness, to become part of the enormous pageant of life played out on its fixed stage. To be in touch, to touch.

In ancient Athens the Agora was the meeting place. Philosophers, peddlers, playwrights and princes came together in daily life to buy the choicest figs and to create the "Politics" and "Poetics" which became the basis of our western civilization. Socrates and Aristotle sat together in the Agora, discussing the profound reality of the olive and the olive branch.

The Romans called it Forum, the site of fowl playing and sometimes, foul play. Caesar was murdered there while someone was haggling over the price of apples. Messengers of the gods often circulated in the market; a stranger could be a god in disguise. The cacophony of soothsayers chanting their prophecies, merchants singing their wares, shrilled with a touch of danger: the unknown in the midst of the known.

The medieval market place was host to passion plays, the plague and passing crusaders. In the entourage of many religious pilgrimages was the merchant. He was the original adventurer-explorer, in pursuit of yet another frontier in taste. The quest for new customers led merchants on daring treks across uncharted landscapes; the Spice Route, the Silk Route were trails blazed across history by entrepreneurs going forth in the name of God — and the gourmet. The market place as depot for all the world's diverse sensuality; exotic delicacies brought back, mingling with the homely necessities of life. Marco Polo carried home spaghetti from China; his countrymen claimed pasta for their own.

Renaissance Man was a merchant. The new product he discovered was HIMSELF; he could package his inner resources to achieve his personal destiny. Bursting with the sudden pride of self-discovery, he became godlike in recognizing his own ingenuity. Michelangelo, selecting a chisel amid the maze of artisans' stalls, was anointed by the splash of splendid fountains in the Florentine square. And this public place, the site of his daily life, became the sacred place. From this sacred market place also sprang forth the Medicis, deriving their power from the Market and their nobility from their own enormous sense of SELF. These Renaissance merchants demanded of their Michelangelos that they tailor God to their own measure. This glorification of the secular life made inevitable the new struggle between Church and State; Savonarola and sweet cakes in the piazza of Florence — each for a price, a price for each.

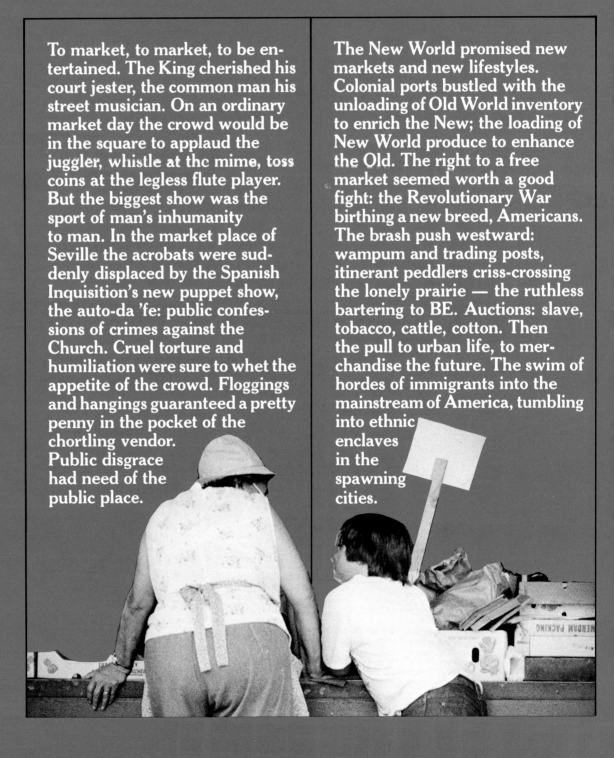

To market, to market, to be entertained. The King cherished his court jester, the common man his street musician. On an ordinary market day the crowd would be in the square to applaud the juggler, whistle at the mime, toss coins at the legless flute player. But the biggest show was the sport of man's inhumanity to man. In the market place of Seville the acrobats were suddenly displaced by the Spanish Inquisition's new puppet show, the auto-da 'fe: public confessions of crimes against the Church. Cruel torture and humiliation were sure to whet the appetite of the crowd. Floggings and hangings guaranteed a pretty penny in the pocket of the chortling vendor. Public disgrace had need of the public place.

The New World promised new markets and new lifestyles. Colonial ports bustled with the unloading of Old World inventory to enrich the New; the loading of New World produce to enhance the Old. The right to a free market seemed worth a good fight: the Revolutionary War birthing a new breed, Americans. The brash push westward: wampum and trading posts, itinerant peddlers criss-crossing the lonely prairie — the ruthless bartering to BE. Auctions: slave, tobacco, cattle, cotton. Then the pull to urban life, to merchandise the future. The swim of hordes of immigrants into the mainstream of America, tumbling into ethnic enclaves in the spawning cities.

Crowded cities, in the twentieth century, becoming voracious, swallowing up the countryside; urban life, tense, intense, impersonal, growing more so. Many old ways of life, getting in the way of that new life, had to be crushed. The teeming neighborhood market, spilling into the street — off the back of a pushcart, out of a barrel, against the curb — had to be tamed by the Machine Age. Such huckstering was deemed uncivilized. Clear the streets of their markets! But valiant defenders, invoking its long history, adapted the Markethouse to the bigness of city. Adorned with a sensible new roof, hemmed in a bit by widening streets, inhibited by Weights and Measures, and now shackled with a modern vocabulary: refrigeration, sanitation, immunization. The market place/meeting place, as American as apple pie — as American as kuchen and kielbasa — was fated to survive.

Slightly stifled, but still sturdy, the Markethouse held its own for a while in the hardening heart of the burgeoning metropolis. The sacred place continued to survive because there was an enduring need for its most precious commodity: the festivity of Market, the activity embraced. The good-natured bantering, the chance to emote. Being expected at a given hour by the butcher who has saved the special chop. Being known in the Markethouse by what you want: you are The Man Who Loves Mushrooms. The extravagance of preparation for the holiday, the feastday. Seeking and finding the rare spice, the elegant roast, the perfect melon. Sharing the family recipe with the woman next in line. The easy access to each other, the choreography of meandering pace. No way to stay a stranger in this sanctuary, this dense familiar place.

Like the bald eagle, the great urban market has become an endangered species in the American landscape, chased from its natural habitat by our advancing mechanized society. But, happily, there are the few survivors, and in these cool, computered times there still exists a Market place where real people push and shove. They yell and laugh and care about each other. They try to give each other what they need: the time of day, the touch of hands, something for their money. The sign outside reads: WEST SIDE MARKET. Come by yourself, you're not alone. Bring the kids, they don't know what it's like in here. Bring Grandma, the old-timers were kids once in this place.

Come on inside, discover for yourself why people hang around here, won't let this bustling Market close. Maybe it's the seduction of such sour and sweet smells. Sauerkraut by the barrel, sausage by the yard; the acrid whiff of sheep's milk cheese, the stabbing scent of candied ginger send you reeling passionately, trying to push closer. The closeness of the place is part of what you love. It doesn't matter what you want — you'll find it here.

Generations of fathers and sons and mothers and daughters have stood guard over this Market with their work ethic, their toughness, their view of the world and especially their sense of belonging. These vendors are not all nice guys. Some drink too much, some slip you rotten apples. But, they greet you by **your name!** You are expected here. You arrive, eager for the give and take, the good-natured jostling. And every Market day becomes a holiday.

To find the West Side Market, look for the clock tower. Thrusting above the urban landscape like a lighthouse out of water, the tower rises almost 150 feet from the sidewalk to hover over the vaulted roof of the Markethouse. The covered arcades of outdoor stalls run along the north flank of the enormous building, then take a right turn to frame the activity of the loading docks. Inside and outside, nearly 200 stands are crammed with every imaginable edible.

The tower stands as an audacious landmark, exclaiming the importance of the public Markethouse. Elegant herringboned brickwork decorates the shaft beneath the clock; a copper dome tops off the beacon which has guided devout generations to the Markethouse.

From the beginning, this was a market site, long before the building was established. Paths hacked across the uncharted Western Reserve intersected here on the river bank. Pioneer farmers dragged slaughtered carcasses to trade, staining with commerce this spot in the wilderness. Land was portioned out, people settled. Paths becoming lanes, becoming streets — laid out, erased, redrawn. For over 200 years the Market Square has been held safe — documented first in handwritten family deeds, then notarized in civic documents.

Just below the clock a narrow ledge girds the great square tower. From that precarious aerie you get the view across the Cuyahoga River to the skyline of downtown Cleveland. The great Market place is tied to the heart of the city by a fretwork of bridges spanning the Cuyahoga River Valley below. Looking out to that grim industrial valley you learn what made nineteenth century Cleveland a lure for countless immigrants seeking the new chance. The river and the great lake combine in the ideal setting for the mills, factories and foundries, pulling hordes of hope-filled workers across the oceans, as they answered the siren's sweet call to a better life.

The word went out in every tongue: Come, build your new life here. But the new life had to be seasoned with something of the old. Please, where can I find oregano, juniper berries, the garlic sausage I need to hold my family together? These comestibles are unknown here? Step forward, sausage maker; step forward, baker; step forward, old woman hording herbs in your knotted kerchief. Grind the spiced pork, knead the hefty black bread, plant the precious seed. To market, to market. Soon it will be found here.

Today, this Market place is completely out of sync with modern life. Don't these vendors know their lifestyle is obsolete? Who ever heard of someone getting up at three o'clock on a dank morning to bid on the choicest melons? The son doing the job because the old man can't load the truck anymore. No air-conditioning, never a vacation, not once in a whole lifetime. Nothing packaged in advance. The custom cutting, the weighing, wrapping, the tying the parcel with **string!**

It gradually becomes clear that the West Side Market has its own clock: everyone in it is living within a time warp. The clock in the tower looms large. It sings out the forgotten time, protecting against change. Sheltered under the glinting dome, its four faces caressed by huge bronze hands, the clock in its tower marks defiance: the folks in here cheerfully choose to ignore the humming, humorless world outside.

They invite you to linger long enough to hear some of their stories, these families who think they can go right on ticking to their own clock. So, come inside. To enter into this Market is to join in an ancient dance. The almost-remembered ritual step, the strangely familiar dissonances, pulling you in toward your vague sense of belonging. And, you do belong — because you have always been here.

The clock in the tower, which has cast its spell over generations of Market people, was designed by the famous Seth Thomas Clock Company. It was an eight-day clock and, until the extensive modernization of the Markethouse in the 1950s, had to be hand-wound every week. Who performed this task?

A small, white haired man waits on the balcony above the foodhall, carefully straightening his collar along the edge of his cardigan sweater. Standing nearly five feet, one inch tall, "Little Charlie" Bisesi beams shyly, acknowledging that he is indeed the person who used to wind the tower clock.

This Quasimodo of the West Side Market offers to escort the visitor on a pilgrimage to the top to visit the clock. Jangling a big ring of keys he scurries along a narrow passageway that runs off the balcony. He climbs a short flight of stairs, stopping in front of a small wooden door patched with rough boards nailed across. The scarred and battered door bears silent testimony to the real danger that the door can slam shut, leaving the intrepid intruder to kick his way out.

Little Charlie wedges the door open with some old paint cans and crosses the worn threshold into the somber open shaft. The elegant tower, soaring outside for all the world to see, is a hollow dungeon here inside. Looking up from the vantage point on the cement floor it is impossible to penetrate the glum darkness to see the cupola at the top.

A gigantic openwork metal stairway zig-zags through the dreary void. Charlie leads the ascent, clanking up the erector-set staircase and as he begins the climb he tells his story.

"When you know a job has got to be done and you do it, there's no reason to feel bad about it. You do it, then it becomes a part of you. That clock was a part of me."

CHARLIE BISESI

I have always been ahead of time. I don't think in the 36 years that I worked for the Market that I was ever late once. Always an hour ahead of time. The Market opened for the tenants at five in the morning, but I used to get here at four. Another reason to come early: you beat the traffic.

I started to work for the City of Cleveland, Division of Markets, in 1934. I worked first at the old Central Market, which is where I got my name, "Little Charlie." It was because of "Big Frank" that I got my name. He was **big**, and when he and I used to walk down the aisles he would walk first and I would be behind him. Nobody could see me until we had passed by. To this day, "Little Charlie" is how everyone knows me.

Old Central Market wasn't built solid like this one and people were always worried it was going to be torn down. But Big Frank always said, "This market will be here as long as I'm here." Well, we buried Big Frank at nine o'clock on a Saturday morning. At nine that same night, Central Market burned down. Somebody had left a heater lit or something. Everybody said, "Well, Big Frank took the market with him!" But, they misunderstood him. He only meant the market would be there as long as he was — not that it would go when he was buried. But, he was gone and it was gone.

The next week I was transferred here, to the West Side Market. Here is where I worked for the rest of my life. There were three of us janitors inside, or "laborers," as we were called. Another crew worked downstairs. Our pride was in keeping the Market in a clean and sanitary condition so that foodstuffs could be sold. Anything that could be done, we did it. That meant sweeping and hosing down the Market floor, taking out the rubbish from behind the stands, scrubbing, polishing. At night we would have to sweep the whole Market before we went home.

You got used to your work and you knew it had to be done. Winding the clock was just one of my jobs. Well, it wasn't so bad. It was an eight-day clock and it had to be wound up once a week, every Monday. There are over 180 steps to climb. First a couple dozen steps to the tower door. Then, once inside the tower, about 150 steps up to the top where the clock is. The original steps were iron and much steeper than the ones that are here now, curling around and around like a big potato peel.

Also, the tower housed an old reservoir — a big water tank that they used to flush out the Market, or in case of fire. It took up an enormous space at the top, but it was disconnected and scrapped for war materials. Now there's nothing inside the tower, just a big open space with the metal stairs. The clock is in a little room of its own at the very top, which you still enter by crawling up a runged fireman's ladder through a narrow tunnel. Each of the four faces of the clock worked from a central winding. There were a lot of wheels and weights. I wound the mechanism with a crank. I mean it's a long hike up to the top where that clock lives.

Right below the clock faces there are doors that open onto a ledge running around the outside of the tower. The ledge is not more than a foot wide and the pigeons would roost there. One of my jobs while I was up there was to clean off what we called the "pigeonitis," which is pigeon droppings. I would open the doors and scrape off all that goop so it wouldn't pile up too much. I used to go out on that ledge and then look down to the street below. I always notified somebody when I was going up, and I warned them that if they didn't see me in 20 minutes to a half hour to make sure to come up and see what's what! The doors could swing shut and lock and I could be stuck out on the ledge over 130 feet up in the air. Of course, I could always holler down and wave, and people would eventually see me.

Well, like I say, it was a living and it was a must; it had to be done. In our days, you had to work to stay alive. So, you got used to that, to the working. When you know a job has got to be done and you do it, there's no reason to feel bad about it. You do it, then it becomes a part of you. That clock was a part of me.

Then something happened. It was my son's first day at the Market. My 14-year-old son, Donald, was working for one of the butchers and on his lunch hour he wanted to come up with me and see the clock. He had never been up before.

So we started up those old iron steps that were very, very steep, going around and around. I was in front of my son and when I got to the very last step up there at the very top, the step broke! It just gave way; probably rusted out. It was a good thing the step was on the **inside,** against the tower wall. If it had been the step on the outside curve, I would have fallen down about 130 feet to the bottom of the tower.

Well, we still had a job to finish so we climbed inside the clock and wound the works. Then we eased our way back down those broken stairs.

I went straight into the Commissioner's

Little Charlie gives a sentimental touch-up to the clock atop the tower.

office. I laid the key to the tower on Mr. Jurowski's desk and I said, "NO MORE WINDING THE CLOCK!" Soon after that, the steps were replaced with these easier metal steps. But the clock was never wound again. Later, it was changed into an electric clock.

So, time goes on. Today the clock is electronically controlled from the Commissioner's office. There's no need to climb up anymore; everything is automatic. I have been replaced by a computer!

Time flies, the world changes. But, some things just can't change. Take me, for instance. Even though I'm retired from the Market these many years, I still get up at three every morning. I'm so used to getting up early to be ahead of time. I'm still like a clock that needs to be wound.

When I go to bed at night, I ask the Lord to let me live one more day. This way, the Lord, when He hears that, He says, "This man is only asking for **one** day — we'll give it to him!"

But, I make sure that I ask Him for that one more day **every night** before I go to sleep.

Little Charlie ascending the clock tower stairway.

The Markethouse occupies a full city block with its massive clock tower squaring off the busy intersection of West 25th and Lorain Avenue. Along the wide expanse of West 25th Street, harsh city life prevails. The Discount Shoe Bazaar slashes the prices on vinyl cowboy boots; the Amigo Bodega flaunts ceramic Madonnas in a wide selection of colors. Occupying the ground floor of a stately nineteenth century building, Gray's Discount Drugs displays disposable diapers bathed in a fluorescent glow. The murky peep-hole of Bender's Bar flashes "Schlitz;" the upstairs windows of the empty buildings are boarded shut.

Down the block, elderly citizens languish, imprisoned in a new high-rise housing unit. On market days some old people venture out through the shabby, already-cracking lobby, shuffling in pairs, painfully working their way along the crowded sidewalk to reach the Markethouse where they will find someone who remembers them. They pass the storefront parlor of the Palm Reader Spiritualist. La Mia Grocery and the Mideast Food Store purr with guttural gossiping. Outside the used-furniture exchange two old women hold each other by the hand, stepping carefully around the rolls of remnant carpet and linoleum lying like fallen Doric pillars.

Sidling up to the hectic frontline of West 25th Street are small, quiet streets: Bridge, Church, Jay, Vestry, Market. Their plain names bespeak another time. The district is called Ohio City and boasts of the oldest church and some of the earliest urban dwellings in these parts. Blight has eaten away big chunks, but the mixed neighborhood that has survived is in the throes of an intensive restoration.

Small century-old brick houses are being tilted upright, razed inside. Abandoned grain and feed warehouses now feed fashionable patrons on crepes and steak tartare. Savvy outsiders proclaim this dilapidation **chic**. Poor middle-Europeans, nervous Hispanics, out-of-work transients sit grimly on their frail front porches and watch the toney rehabilitation of the ruins that, by default, had belonged to them.

No matter what lifestyle emerges from this urban renewal struggle, the pull of the neighborhood continues to be toward Market Square. The traditional space in front of the Markethouse is marked off with a small park designed as a resting place in the midst of the commercial din. On benches maintained by the City, old women sit inventorying their shopping bags and homeless bums lie out, perhaps dreaming of a sweeter time, when vendors hawked live chickens in the square and offered fresh-cut flowers.

There are many entrances into the Markethouse: the main facade on West 25th Street offers four sets of doors, multiple sets of doors punctuate the two long sides of the building, and the vendors and employees use the loading docks across the back end. Above each of the many doorways, granite lintels balance sets of stone rosettes depicting a variety of Market offerings: fruit, fowl, fish.

A man in a tan windbreaker pausing on the curb across the street tips on his heels to look up at the clock in the tower. Out of habit, he checks the reading on his watch against the giant clock. The traffic light changes and he crosses the street, heading for the tower entrance at the corner. In a hurry, he pulls open the heavy door and does not notice the ornate decorations suspended from the pointed archway: a covey of quail on the left and a family of rabbits carved nicely on the right.

Just inside the door one is assaulted by griddle vapors wafting from the hot dog stand along the left wall. This street-level slice of the tower, handsomely encased in white tilework, serves as the vestibule of the great Markethouse. Above the tiled ceiling looms the unseen vast interior of the tower, rising in gloom to the clock cupola.

Beyond the vestibule the cigar stand fills the corner to the right of the door which leads into the food halls. This sentry booth, constructed of old wooden display cases, is heavily encrusted with candy bars, packs of chewing gum, cough drops, chewing tobacco.

Standing guard inside this bunker is John Tricsko, gatekeeper of the West Side Market. For more than 35 years John has owned and operated the cigar stand. From behind the counters, stockpiled with boxes of cigars, cheap lighters and tobacco pouches, he has observed the daily comings and goings in the Market. Above John's head an illuminated display of pipes flickers bleakly. The corn cob pipes and pre-smoked stems stapled in angled juxtapositions read like a mysterious hieroglyph in an ancient coat-of-arms. The wall behind John is a mosaic of cigarette packs in open cartons. Tiers of magazines, newspapers and comic books form a patchwork skirt in front of the stand. Fanning out neatly on the counter top are several foreign language weeklies: "Szabadsag," "Gwiazda Polarna," "Wächter und Anzeiger."

John Tricsko, gatekeeper of the Markethouse, was born right around the corner on Church Street; for most of his life he has straddled the few blocks between Market and home. His wife, Mary, the small pretty woman almost hidden behind the futuristic machine that issues State Lottery tickets, has lived in the neighborhood since she was a teenager. She mans the massive blue computer like a pioneer wife at the stockades.

Mary and John and their five children live in the house that was originally her mother's; a restored 1898 mansion around the corner on Vestry. At any given moment, several members of the Tricsko family can easily be located somewhere within the tight circumference drawn by the house and cigar stand.

"Living in this neighborhood and working in the Market has spoiled us for any other way of life."

THE TRICSKO FAMILY

MARY: My life began in this Market back in 1935 when my mother, who was a widow, bought the hot dog stand. I would help out at the hot dog stand after school and on Saturdays. There were no paper dishes in those days; we had to wash every cup and every plate, including those heavy root beer mugs. A hot dog was a nickel; a hamburger was a nickel, too.

At that time the Market was open until eleven on Saturday nights. We lived way out near Kamm's Corners and after the long Market day we would have to wait for the streetcar, often not getting home until after midnight, completely exhausted. The convenience of being able to walk to our business meant a lot to the two of us, so my mother bought the old house on Vestry.

John and his family were living right down the block; it was strange how we met. The doorbell in the house broke and it seemed no one knew how to repair it. My mother even called over the electrician from the Market, but it would not work for anybody. An elderly neighbor mentioned to my mother that there was a family down the block with some boys who were so handy at fixing things.

JOHN: That's right. The old man told us, "There's a widow up at the corner, and her doorbell won't work!"

MARY: I think John was sort of pushed into being the one to check the doorbell; the other boys refused to come, and he **did** fix the doorbell. By the way, it still works.

JOHN: The war broke out just about the time that Mary and I decided to get married. There were four boys at home and none of us had been called. So, my brother Louie went down to the draft board to ask what his chances were of being drafted. He went down and they drafted him! I told Mary that I was going down just to

inquire how I stood, so we could decide about getting married. It was May 1st — I'll never forget little whitehaired Mr. Cracken. He was so sympathetic, so kind. He told me not to worry about going to the Army but to make my wedding plans. So, he took my papers and threw them on **top** of the big pile on his desk. One week later exactly, May 8th, 1942, I was in Camp Perry, Ohio. I came home on a furlough and we were married anyway.

MARY: When John came home from the Army in 1944, the opportunity to buy the cigar stand came up. The Geschwind family had owned the stand since the turn of the century — originating in the old wooden market across the street. When Mr. Geschwind died, his wife and sons pitched in. It was a struggle to earn a living so they ran a little gambling on the side: dice games, punch boards, horse racing.

When old Mrs. Geschwind was ready to retire, anyone who inquired about buying the cigar stand was warned that there was to be no gambling! It was against the law, particularly on City property. The Commissioner was eager to have John acquire the stand because he knew there would be no trouble. On December 8, 1944, John took over the business. We have been running the cigar stand for more than 35 years.

JOHN: Living in this neighborhood and working in the Market all these years has spoiled us for any other way of life. Lately, you'd be surprised how many young people are returning from the suburbs, coming back here to Ohio City. None of our kids wants to leave here. They insist that we must never sell our house.

MARY: People tell us they have lived on a street for five years and no one has ever spoken to them. In our neighborhood, that would be impossible: not to know the **names** of people. There is a sense of well-being in knowing each other. That's why so many elderly come to the Market. They certainly don't need a lot anymore in the way of food. They come just to walk around a bit, see the people, say hello. Maybe meet a friend or two. If they have a problem, even if they can't talk about it, they come to the Market and their minds are occupied; they're not thinking about their trouble. Right there a problem is solved!

JOHN: My mother is 88 years old and sharp as a bullet. Now she lives way out with my sister, but she loves coming down to the Market. She tells me it's just like coming into heaven! She goes around and buys little odds and ends. The merchants take care of these old-timers, whether they buy or not.

MARY: John's mother always tells us that we don't know how lucky we are to be here. When she lived in this neighborhood, if **all she needed** was a quart of milk, well, it was **fun** to go to the Market to buy it. Now, if she needs a quart of milk, someone has to take her in the car to a store to buy it. There is no pleasure in it for her anymore.

I've been in the Markethouse for nearly 45 years and I can't say that I'm tired of it. You form an attachment to this place, by working here, by shopping here. Once you get inside the door, you catch this incurable disease — you know it's hopeless. You can't get away from the Market.

JOHN: And there is always something **happening** in the Market. The word gets passed along from stand to stand: "Hey, do you know what's happening?" Once, there were a couple of men who dressed up as nuns and they were circulating around, trying to collect as much money as they could from the merchants and customers. Someone noticed the beard on one of them and then someone saw the men's shoes. The chase was on! They ran out of the Markethouse, their long dresses flying. It's always something.

MARKET
HOUSE
HISTORY

WHEN the West Side Markethouse was dedicated in 1912, it was heralded as the grandest and most modern facility of its kind in the world. But this lofty public foodhall took some getting used to. At first, some were a bit shy in the place, yearning for its predecessor — the decrepit wooden Pearl Street Markethouse with its primitive stalls and sawdust covered earthen floors.

The old Pearl Street Market, built in 1868 on the corner of Lorain Avenue and Pearl Street (later renamed West 25th Street), was the first public market on a site designated as "Market Square." In 1840, two early settlers of Ohio City, Josiah Barber and Richard Lord, had given the tract of land with the condition that it always be kept as a public market site. The land was incorporated into the City of Cleveland in 1856; the stipulation is respected to the present day. In the earliest days open-air farmers' markets flourished — the first known of these street markets was established on Ontario Street in 1829 — and by 1837, when Cleveland was one year old, four were listed on the public records. Before the building of the Pearl Street Market, Ohio City settlers frequented the open-air market on Franklin Place, a large circle of land platted by the county and dedicated to the public in 1836.

As the community developed, the Markethouse became the lifeline for many newly-arrived immigrants who stopped first at the Market, where they were sure to find others speaking their language to help them through the difficult initiation into American life. How to find a job, a wife, a doctor, a place to live — somebody in the Market could surely help. The Market place as sanctuary.

Some immigrant families tried their luck at being vendors, bringing the produce to Market in horse-drawn wagons, arriving to set up in the middle of the night, the children usually tucked in among the cabbages and onions. Many personal dreams got crushed beneath the potatoes, the melons; survival of the family took precedence over a son's or daughter's private ambitions.

By the turn of the century, the old kerosene lighted, one-story wooden Pearl Street structure was losing its charm and was no longer adequate to serve the needs of the growing population. It was too primitive, too small, too unsanitary — and highly flammable. Mayor Tom L. Johnson appointed a Market Commission and in 1902 the City authorized bonds for the purchase of seven parcels of land to accommodate a modern facility. In 1905 the Bureau of Public Service of the City of Cleveland contracted with the architectural firm of Hubbell and Benes to construct a public Markethouse on the southwest corner of Lorain Avenue and West 25th Street at a cost of $680,000 in public monies.

The concept, avant-garde for its time, called for a multifunctional complex of buildings, much like the civic centers filling the cores of major cities in contemporary America. The original plans, later

The old wooden
Pearl Street
Market.

vetoed, featured a separate 5,000-seat auditorium and a two-story building facing the projected Markethouse containing public comfort stations, a flower market and public baths. (As late as the 1920s it was still considered to be the City's responsibility to provide public bath houses because of the lack of indoor plumbing in scattered neighborhoods.)

The architects chosen to build the new West Side Markethouse were two men who complemented each other. W. Dominick Benes was born in Prague, Czechoslovakia, in 1857 and came to Cleveland as a young immigrant. He attended Oberlin Academy but left after the second year to study architecture under an uncle in Chicago, an informal apprenticeship common in the 19th century. By contrast, Charles Hubbell, a native of Leavenworth, Kansas, received formal training, earning his master's degree in architecture from Cornell University in 1894. The Hubbell and Benes partnership was formed in 1897 and this highly respected firm went on to contribute significantly to architecture in Cleveland. Besides the West Side Markethouse, they designed the Cleveland Museum of Art, the Central YMCA at Prospect and East 22nd Streets, and the Illuminating Company Building on Public Square. The Wade Memorial Chapel which they designed in Lakeview Cemetery is admired as a classic of its kind.

Hubbell and Benes sought inspiration for their Markethouse in public places down through history — the Roman Coliseum, basilicas (places for pubic congregation), and in more modern prototypes such as railroad stations and armories. Through his formal training, Hubbell was well versed in the Beaux Arts vocabulary of architectural styles and particularly adept in the use of classical design elements. Benes, on the other hand, had learned from experience what it meant to build a

Excavating
the site for
the new
Markethouse, 1907.

9-13-07
4-20 P.M.

practical building. This partnership then was uniquely equipped to face the challenge of designing a public foodhall.

The new Markethouse had to fulfill these descriptions:

inviting — diverse groups of people would come flocking in from widespread areas;

economical — its construction was being financed with public monies through bond issues;

fireproof — codification of City regulations came in the early 1900s;

The Markethouse
begins to
take form, 1909.

hygienic — its special function was the purveying of
perishable foodstuffs;

easy and inexpensive to maintain — it would be in
continuous use and in need of constant cleaning; and

durable — it would be subjected to daily hard wear
and long-term activity.

How did Hubbell and Benes resolve these
issues? A careful study of how they met these chal-
lenges is the fascinating architectural story of the
West Side Markethouse. The place of public con-

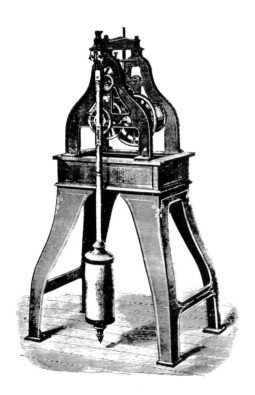

Drawing
from an old
Seth Thomas
Clock Company
catalogue
featuring the
works for the
eight-day
tower clock.

gregation which they designed is a monument to beauty and pragmatism and has been recognized and honored for these aspects through its designation as a Landmark on the National Register of Historic Buildings.

The clock tower of the Markethouse evokes a set pattern of experiences, for a tower defines the upper limits of space, and in a city-scape, is the point of orientation for the surrounding neighborhoods. When first built, this dramatic lighthouse shone for miles around; glimpsed from a distance, it was a beacon reassuring the visitor that he was traveling in the right direction. Its 137-foot thrust was significantly higher than any structure around it, but today, eclipsed by highrises and the rush of vehicular traffic, it seems somewhat diminished.

As the visitor approaches, his eye travels from the large base up the four-sided, gently tapered column with its diagonals of diaper patterned brickwork and stops at the horizontal band of cornices. The clocks above the decorative balustrades of the protruding cornices are a point of interest holding the eye before it continues upward to view the copper dome of the cupola, which at one time was topped with a finial.

The tower originally housed an enormous steel water tank which supplied the water necessary for flushing out the Markethouse. The independent gravity-pressured tank probably compensated for a low pressure City water supply at the time. During

World War II the tank was dissassembled for scrap metal.

The clock so grandly ensconced in the tower was designed by A.S. Hotchkiss and manufactured by the Seth Thomas Clock Company of Thomastown, Connecticut, one of two companies that gained fame specializing in the production of tower clocks. A perusal of old Seth Thomas catalogues dating back to the 1800s reveals a treasure-trove of information about the precision and artistry involved in the manufacture of these clocks. Almost every church, court house, city hall or civic building in America sported a Seth Thomas clock. Independence Hall in Philadelphia features a centennial tower clock produced by the Seth Thomas Company in 1875.

The model installed in the West Side Market tower was an eight-day non-striking timepiece. It was hand-wound once a week until 1954, when the original works were replaced by remote-controlled electronic mechanisms. Despite its accommodation to modern technology, the clock in the tower continues to cast its spell over the throngs of people who pause before entering the Markethouse to confirm the time.

The conservation of any tower is a chronic problem and the maintenance of the West Side Market tower has been no exception. There were considerations given to tearing the tower down at one time, but in a change of heart, the City of Cleveland and the Tenants' Association invested

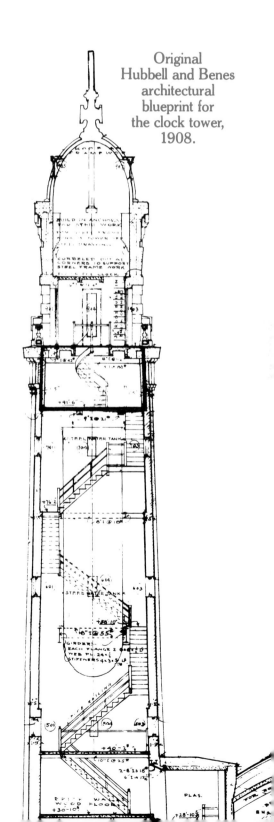

Original Hubbell and Benes architectural blueprint for the clock tower, 1908.

The Markethouse
interior
showing the
marble-countered
vendors' stands,
circa 1913.

over one million dollars in 1954 for extensive renovation of the tower and the Markethouse. Almost
twenty years later, in 1973, large sections of the
cornice had seriously deteriorated and created an
emergency problem when a piece of the tile from just
below the clock balcony broke off and fell on the
street below. This time there was a bit of irony
involved in the repair.

The original blueprints reveal that the
ornamental work at the base of the cupola was
intended to be made of granite. But an exchange of

View down
Abbey Street
to the
Markethouse tower
before the clock
was installed,
circa 1911.

querulous letters in June and July of 1909 between the architects and the Woodbury Granite Company in Hardwick Vermont, reflects the quarry's dissatisfaction with the incomplete specifications sent to them, threatening expensive delays in cutting the stone. At that point, the architects slid around the problem and completed the work with terracotta, a cheaper material. This change in the specifications came back to haunt Berj Shakarian (now the Cuyahoga County Architect) 64 years later.

Shakarian was contracted for the repair work on the deteriorated sections in 1973; his plans called for replacing the now-extinct terracotta with granite. However, because the Markethouse had recently been entered on the National Register of Historic Places as a Landmark, it was subject to the strict guidelines for restoration of an historic structure. Because terracotta had been used in the original construction it had to be used in the restoration. Fortunately, the City had chosen the right man for the job. Shakarian took on the project with a loving commitment to restore rather than simply to repair the tower.

He field-checked all the original work and researched the composition and color of the tiles — which he found to be a buff color of Eastern European baroque origin — and finally contracted with a factory in California to custom produce the tiles. His masterful recreation of upper sections of the tower led to professional recognition and a builder's award in 1978, and this appealing landmark was saved for the continuing pleasure of generations of market-goers.

There are subtle ways in which the Markethouse invites us to come in. The tower itself, sitting on the southwest corner, breaks the symmetry of the central building and creates a relaxed feeling. The exterior facade of yellow brick gives off a warm, inviting tone as opposed to the serious gray stone of more formal edifices. A variety of approaches to the Markethouse accommodates the diverse routes fol-

lowed by the many people coming to Market. The
outdoor food arcades running along one side of the
building extends the assymmetry and reinforces the
relaxed mood. This non-authoritarian mood is
appropriate for a Markethouse as contrasted with
the very symmetrical and formal front stairs that
serve as an entree to such buildings as the City Hall.

Entering the Markethouse through one of

the many doors on Lorain Avenue on the south or through the produce arcades on the north, a visitor passes first into one of the low-ceilinged side aisles. If he continues directly on through to the main hall, he is sure to be startled, for the vaulted ceiling, hovering 44 feet overhead, shelters a central concourse nearly the size of the arena of the Roman Coliseum, running 241 feet in length and 124 feet across. The food stands cluster in quadrangles, intersected by aisles in both directions. The experience of emerging from the lower side aisles makes the central space seem even larger than it is. This sumptuous food emporium, flaunting the sheer volume of its captured space, arouses excitement every time it is visited.

The reasons that the architects devised this shift in space were two-fold: it would have cost more to build it with a single, wide span; and immediate entry into the interior would have ruined the visual surprise. Thus, the basilica plan reconciled both economic and aesthetic considerations. However, in meeting the specifications for 100 stands inside the Markethouse it was inevitable, with this format, that some stands would be more desirable in location and size than others. This problem was overcome by drawing numbers out of a hat when the original tenants were being assigned their stands in 1912. The rent was commensurate with the desirability of the stands' locations.

The vast tiled interior of the central Market concourse provides an ideal and exciting space for the throngs of shoppers who have passed through for almost 70 years. The arched walls faced with white tile rise 25 feet to a clerestory which joins the tile ceiling, 44 feet high at its highest point. The flow of the ceiling is interrupted by five beams from which the ceiling vaults spring.

Tiles were the perfect solution to the building requirements of a public Markethouse: inexpensive, lightweight, non-porous, and prefabricated. Their hard white surfaces reflect light and symbolize cleanliness. As if to emphasize the modest atmosphere, the tiles were left exposed rather than plastered over with decorative work. They are practically indestructible, as evidenced by the fact that much of what we know of antiquity is through the study of terracotta shards unearthed as markers in time. In fact, the quarry tiles of the floor are in virtually the same condition today as when they were laid down.

Because the ceilings were made of tiles and were therefore relatively light, the supporting walls could be less massive, allowing the wide arched openings and many windows for natural light. Despite provision for very up-to-date electrical lights running in rows down the tiled beams and around the ceiling vents, natural lighting was central to the Market's design. Light flooded in through the windows of the clerestory, the side aisles, and before the murals were installed, through the windowed arches of the east and west ends. Natural light is ever-changing and thus psychologically more interesting as opposed to the constant and artificial light in a supermarket.

For purposes of Market life, the tiles serve another important role: the hard glazed surface of the walls and ceiling acts as a giant sound reflector. A huge interior shell of tile and glass such as the Market's provides tremendous acoustical excitement, the excitement of "going to Market." The vivacious character of the walls create a mood akin to singing in the shower, for the shopper has an irrepressible urge to add to the lively din.

The original ventilation and heating systems were based largely on environmental effects. The ventilation system employed is the medieval "chimney" effect. Air comes in through the windows and doors, flows up through the round ventilating registers of each ceiling vault and into the hollow attic space above the ceiling. It then goes on over and out the copper shields of the ventilating louvre on the roof. A 30-inch fan in the west end of the attic pulls air up from the restrooms in the basement through a meandering vent duct, blowing it on through the roof-top louvre. Because of the large crowds circulating through the Markethouse and the natural heat that they generate, only a minimal heating system was provided for cold weather months.

A study of the architects' blueprints reveals the layout for the other facilities of the Markethouse. A mezzanine runs along the west end; off to the right are rooms originally designated as an apartment with livingroom, dining room and kitchen. On the left side of the mezzanine is office space. The east end on the ground floor level gives access to the base-

A spectacular feature of the Markethouse interior: the Gustavino tiled ceiling.

ment and cold storage areas with staircases and freight elevators; general office space is on the second story over the loading docks. On either side of the east end are identical rooms — a fish market on the north side and a restaurant on the Lorain Avenue side.

The basement houses the vast cold storage area with individual coolers, a boiler room, pump room, compressor room, tank room, generator room and public toilets. The cooling and heating facilities underwent extensive modernization in 1954 when the City invested $1.1 million in a renovation program including the installation of modern refrigeration and heating systems.

From the day the Markethouse opened its doors in 1912 until today, a visitor is sure to gawk at the splendid ceiling of the central hall. The tile vaulting is a patented system of vaulting called "Guastavino." A forerunner of the modern concrete shell, this age-old Mediterranean system of erecting thin masonry vaults was brought to this country in 1881 from Spanish Catalonia, where it was called a "Catalan" vault, by the Guastavino father and son, both named Raphael. Their introduction of this technique to America made possible the Old World spatial effects created in many of the "blue ribbon" buildings designed in the late 19th and early 20th centuries.

The vault is very thin and derives its rigidity from the fact that it is curved in two directions, like the surface of an egg. The tiles are laid flat with the curve of the vault, usually in two or more layers, and in a diagonal pattern (a herringbone pattern in the Markethouse). The tiles are held together by a thick blanket of mortar so tenacious that tiles will ordinarily break or split before the mortar parts. The whole becomes a sort of concrete made with mortar and pieces of tile.

The Markethouse ceiling has a six-foot high clear space above the vaults and because these vaults can support tremendous weight, maintenance workers are able to work on the ventilating and power equipment by walking around in the space.

There were other advantages to the Guastavino system of tile vaulting:

the vault is very light weight in comparison with ordinary stone or brick vaulting;

it can be designed with a very low rise because it exerts very little lateral thrust;

being composed of terracotta and hydraulic cement, it is completely non-combustible and resistant to the spread of fire (in their promotional materials the Guastavinos emphasized this and called their firm the Guastavino Fireproof Construction Company); and it was remarkably inexpensive.

The Markethouse is, in effect, double-roofed, for the vaulted tile inner roof and attic space above are covered by a pitched red tile outer roof, which serves as a protective — and fireproof — umbrella, shielding the tile ceiling from the elements and hot summer sun.

By the turn of the century the Guastavino tile system was so popular that the father and son were encouraged to set up a tile manufacturing plant in Woburn, Mass., where they developed a wide variety of patented tiles. As the century opened, "Guastavino" became a household word among American architects and the system was incorporated in most building manuals. The height of activity came between the establishment of the Woburn plant and the Depression of the 1930s, and by the time of the Company's retirement in the 1960s, it had installed Catalan-type vaulting in more than

1000 buildings in the United States — many of them landmarks.

Today in the United States the Guastavino tile vault is now extinct as a practiced building system, priced out of existence by the development of concrete shells. The rise in the cost of hand labor, the Great Depression and the development of thin shell concrete structures brought down the enterprise.

There are many decorative elements in the Markethouse; some serve structural devices, most are just for fun. When arriving at the Markethouse from the West 25th Street approach, one can look up to see the splendid cartouche which hides the ventilating louvre on the roof. An eagle with outstretched wings hovers over a pair of cornucopias overflowing with fruits and vegetables. A wreath of acanthus leaves, a Roman civic symbol, encircles the eagle. The iconography of this piece can be read as symbolizing the City's role in providing this public foodhall for the good of all the people.

At the opposite end of the building, above the loading docks, is a very naturalistic cartouche of a cow's head, adding an earthy touch to the busy working end of the Markethouse. Both reliefs were sculpted by Walter Sinz, a Cleveland artist.

All of the decorative elements inside and outside the Markethouse depict items of food. Cast reliefs cap the lintels over each entrance door, offering a moveable feast of lobsters, turtles, cabbages, corn, grapes, fish, pineapples, pigs and sheep running along the sides of the building. There is some duplication of motif, but the four sculptures decorating the pediments of the two tower doors are unique and particularly charming. The west door features game: woodcocks on the left and rabbits on the right. The south door highlights fowl: ducks on the left and a rooster and hen on the right.

Inside the foodhall all the decoration is ceramic, designed and executed by Herman Matzen, the Cleveland sculptor whose best known work is the memorial monument of Mayor Tom L. Johnson on Public Square. The ventilating registers in the ceiling have been treated as works of art, with the enhancement of Della Robbia-style ceramic wreaths encircling rings of lights in each oculus. The finest and most exquisite touches, the decorative corbels on each of five arches, unfortunately have been almost obliterated from view by light panels hanging above each stand (part of the modernization done in 1954). Cast in white ceramic, each of the large reliefs features an animal, fruit or vegetable surrounded and embellished by other fruits of the earth.

The great arched windows at either end of the Markethouse, which originally allowed natural light to flood into the interior, were covered over with murals in 1979 as part of a half-million-dollar renovation project. The mural on the west end is by Nancy Martt and depicts farm animals, fish, and dairy products — all outsized, brightly colored and highly stylized. The east wall is filled by Bob Takatch's huge, colorful mural of fruits and vegetables. The Buddy Simon Sign Company executed

A   B

D

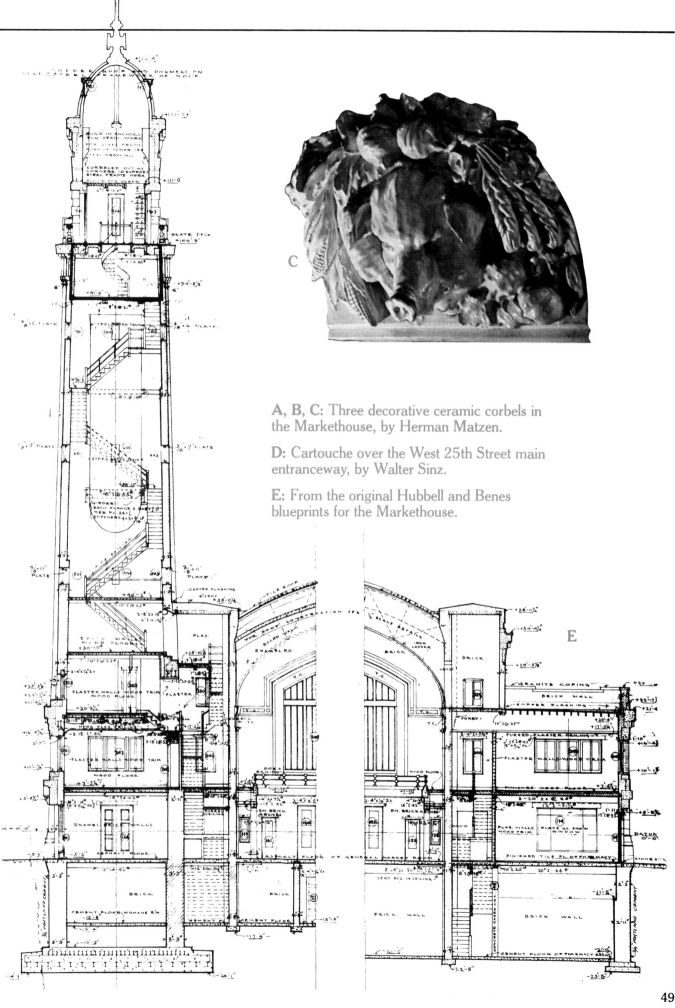

A, B, C: Three decorative ceramic corbels in the Markethouse, by Herman Matzen.

D: Cartouche over the West 25th Street main entranceway, by Walter Sinz.

E: From the original Hubbell and Benes blueprints for the Markethouse.

C

E

the murals, transferring the designs to 20-by-40-foot aluminum panels. John Pilch, Commissioner of the Market, when asked by a newspaper reporter to comment on the artistic merits of the murals, said, "When people ask me why the chicken on the wall is blue, I tell them that the Market only serves blue ribbon chickens, and that seems to satisfy them."

Pedestrians' view of the clock tower looking up from West 25th Street, circa 1912.

Pedestrians'
view of the clock tower
looking up from
West 25th Street,
circa 1981.

RILL
LOUIS SEVERIC
F-6
EMIL CHURCHIN
JOHN ROLSTON
KOCH'S
WALTER F. EHRNFELT
E-4
W.J. KOVALCSIK
FOOD COUPONS
BEE . JAY

Many of the merchant families who sold their wares on opening day in 1912 are still here today. Linked through the generations, they carry on the tradition of offering the family's specialty.

The Stumpf family is among the original vendors who have held their place down through the decades. At the turn of the century Stumpf's homemade sausages were a lure, pulling in the quickly expanding German community who came in droves to savour the tastes they had forfeited in their exodus from the Fatherland.

Every Market day people are jammed together three-deep around their large stand. The homemade bolognas, salamis, cottage hams, smoked turkeys and liverwursts glisten in the display cases. Women hugging cloth shopping bags appraise each other with quick glances, affirming comradeship in their shared knowledge that Stumpf's is the BEST. Someone taps against the glass case to request the triple-smoked Black Forest bacon, elegantly pleated in velvet slices.

Robert, Jr., the youngest brother (he is in his sixties), is the family impresario. He has introduced modern merchandising, presenting the family products under the brand name KITCHEN MAID MEATS. In the Stumpf factory about 40 blocks west of the Market, the sausages are concocted according to secret family recipes. Robert arrives at the factory at daybreak to supervise the grinding, stuffing, smoking. Like a devoted doctor, he tirelessly experiments to improve the quality of their meat products. Brandishing a salami instead of a sword, he leads the crusade against high nitrites.

Every Friday and Saturday he is here behind the counter in the Markethouse, always in motion, wiping his hands across his vast white apron. If you snag him for just half a minute, he will settle his large frame squarely on both feet, shove back his jaunty cloth driving cap to scratch his forehead and launch into a spicy anecdote — garnished with JUST ONE MORE little story to tell why this Market is his life.

THE STUMPF FAMILY:ROBERT STUMPF, JR.

I am a pretty good salesman. My father taught me how to sell. He was a talented German, a very good looking man. His handwriting was beautiful; he attended Heidelberg College for two years and then trained as a pharmacist. When he came over in about 1892,he got into the knitting mills. By the early 1900s he was working for Brookside Sausage down at the old market. Many Germans were attracted to settling in Cleveland because of the famous German singing societies here. My mother and father belonged. On special occasions like Schiller Day, there would be up to three-thousand singers at Edgewater Park; people would come from all over. All the Germans visited my father down at the Market. He was a comedian, a typical good-time Charlie. He enjoyed life, every minute of it.

When he worked for Brookside Sausage, he watched how they did it and then he decided to buy a stand of his own. He was still a pharmacist at heart and he loved using the grams scale, measuring out all the ingredients. In the beginning we had a sausage kitchen at home in the basement. My father loved to drink and many a night when he was too intoxicated to make sausage he would get my brothers and me up in the middle of the night and we would work half the night making sausages. The long Market hours made it an 18-hour day and the family ran the business. Our father was rough, but he taught us a lot. The more lickin's we got, the more we seemed to respect him. But, we lost a lot of our childhood.

One winter day (I must have been seven years old), I had a bad cold and my mother was concerned about my going to the Market. But I **had** to go because we had no hired help to run the stand. My mother knew that on the way home my father would be sure to stop off at several speak-easies. These were Prohibition days and he usually hit three or four places on the way home. My mother lectured me as she was bundling me up that I should not go into the place at night; that if I stayed in the car maybe my father would feel a little bit more compassion and not stay too long. We worked in the cold Markethouse all day and on the way home I felt sick. When my father stopped at the first speak-easy I said, "Hey, Pa, I'm gonna stay in the car — Ma told me to stay in the car." My father said, "You're gonna freeze." It was an old touring car, no heater and it was 15 degrees out.

After about a half hour I was becoming numb. I staggered out of the car; I was stiffer than a board from the cold. I could see down in the basement where several men were singing and drinking. I started down the steps; my shoes were full of snow and down I went. Sliding straight through the door, I landed inside the room. I was so numb that I had to lay there for a few seconds until I could get used to the light. I was really shook up; I looked up at my father. "Pa, I'm frozen." My father glanced in my direction and said, "I **told** you you were gonna freeze." And that was all the compassion he had for me. My father was strict, he was very strict — but this incident is one of the things that I have remembered all my life.

You couldn't blame those men for drinking; the life was so hard. For instance, there were no refrigerated trucks in those days and when the meat came in we had to use gallons of vinegar to wash the stuff off. Vinegar is one of the greatest antibiotics. It kills the bacteria but then it evaporates. It's safe. We had to wash off every piece of meat that was delivered.

When we first had a car down at the Market, it was a problem in the wintertime to keep it warmed up so that it would start. So, in cold weather every couple of hours there was a pilgrimage, led by my father, of a bunch of butchers going out to the parking lot to start up their cars. My father insisted his had to run for

10, 20 minutes. Every time my father came back inside, I could smell alcohol. I would say, "Pa, gee whiz, I smell alcohol." He'd say, "Yeah, that damn radiator is leaking again." They were gone a half-dozen times on a Saturday and they stayed out a good half-hour each trip. Just a beautiful excuse to get out of the stands and have a little companionship.

My father could wait on two or three customers at the same time and keep them all happy. A lady would say, "I want a half-pound of liver sausage." I would aim for a half-pound, making a little game out of seeing how close I could cut it. My father would breeze by me and

Robert Stumpf inspecting a batch of sausages fresh out of his smokehouse.

Robert Stumpf
at work in his
sausage factory.

he'd say under his breath, "Immer **mehr** — always more! Don't you dare cut **under,** and you'd better get **over;** two or three ounces over." He'd tell me, "Two or three hundred customers, two or three ounces over; that is the business." And that is the way you paid for the ends, parts you couldn't sell, and the rent on the stand.

Around 1916, the power in the Markethouse wasn't too dependable and every Saturday the lights would be sure to go out at least a half-dozen times. We always kept candles around and since my father smoked a lot of cigars we had plenty of matches. When the lights would go, it was black in this Market. The stands had flat marble tops which were very sanitary and easy to keep clean but the customers could walk up and touch the merchandise. We had the ring bolognas and the ring sausages all stacked up on the counter, maybe eight or nine high, in artistic piles. There were flocks of women squawking around the Market, all wearing babushkas and all dressed in the same drab clothes, carrying huge baskets. When the lights went out, they would just dart up to the stand and flick a couple of ring bolognas, a cottage ham into their baskets and out they would go. When the lights came back on, you could see what was missing from the display, but you wouldn't know which babushka to chase because they all looked alike. We never caught a single one.

I turned down a scholarship to play basketball for a little college in Illinois because I had to work when I finished high school. But my father had taught me to hate the Market and I vowed that I would never work there again in my life. I decided to try a different career. I went to work in a dress factory and I became a very good dress cutter. After cutting meat, that seemed like an easy life. For five or six years I worked as a dress cutter. But, then, one day, that doggone liver sausage of my father's began to haunt me — that wonderful sausage that I used to hate making. The taste of it came back to me and I just could not resist the urge to be where

that liver sausage was. Its delicious aroma lured me back to the Market.

By then my father had lost his stand at the West Side Market and he was pretty ill from too much drinking. He came to me and said he had a chance to buy another stand in the Market if I would come back with him. It was November 15, 1938, when we bought the stand and opened up. Christmas Eve of the same year he developed double pneumonia and died. So everything was on my shoulders and I just dug in.

If this was going to be my life and I was going to be able to support my wife and children, I had to find a proper place to manufacture my sausages. Somebody told me there was a chance to make a good buy on a piece of property, but I had no money. There was an old German named William Gekster who often came to the stand to visit me. He was a retired brewmaster and would pass the time of day talking about my father, who had been his good friend. The day I got the call about the property, he came by and I must have been looking pretty gloomy. He asked me what was the matter. I told him that the property was going up for auction and that I could get it for about 3,500 dollars. He said, "Yep. You want some money?" I felt pretty low. "Where am I going to get that kind of money, Mr. Gekster?" He said, "Now wait. I'm going to tell you something. I came to this country many years ago and I had twelve children and we didn't have a thing to eat. And somebody told me to go see your father in the Market. Your father gave me a bushel basket full of food to take home to my children." Mr. Gekster looked at me and beamed, "Now, I even the score!" So, we went down to the auction sale and he wrote out a check; he bought the place for me. He gave me the chance. This is how the circle comes.

I paid him off so fast it was amazing. I worked night and day because I had to run both the sausage factory and the stand in the Market.

I loved the life in the Market; what laughs we had about some of the crazy goings-on. The practical jokes that kept us all going. The biggest item for Christmas was the "New York" dressed turkey. That means a turkey with the intestines, the neck, the head and the legs all arranged in place. Years ago, before there was viscerated poultry. every bird had to be killed fresh. Carl Kaufmann, who had the poultry stand, would accumulate a mountain of intestines as the day grew longer. By then the guys had had a few drinks, they were tired and feeling a little nutty. They would get a bag and fill it with 15 pounds of intestines and they would wrap it up real nice. Then they would wedge that turkey head out one end and the legs out the other, which was the proper way to wrap the "New York" turkey. They would set it up on the marble counter, knowing that someone would be sure to swipe it. Invariably, bingo! That thing was gone! They

A vintage collection of faithful Stumpf customers.

must have pulled that gag a dozen times in a day. One time, a guy brought back the stolen goods and threw all the intestines back at Carl! Boy, the laughs we had.

Christmas was big for the poultry men, but New Year's was the big day for us who specialized in pork. The ethnic people all eat pork on New Year's Eve for a very symbolic reason: a chicken scratches **backward** when it feeds, but a pig pushes **forward** when it roots for food. So, the ethnic people like pork for the New Year because it pushes forward.

I decided to call my line **Kitchen Maid** because I wanted to get away from the commercialism of factory-made. I like to keep things more personal. If someone asks for 10 or 15 pounds of frankfurters a little bit longer, I'll say sure. I have to get my sausage man to change the whole set-up on the machine. Now, a big commercial place would laugh at you. Production is all they want. I like production, but I like it with a little enthusiasm from me.

So many of my customers come just to say hello. If I don't show up at my stand, everybody wants to know what happened. There was this one little lady who always came, I think she was Bohemian. "Butcher, Butcher, I want a dollar and a quarter worth of cottage ham." She was in the aisle and she grabbed my hand. So, I cut off a big chunk of cottage ham and put it on the scale. I didn't even look; it was probably two dollar's worth. About two weeks later, she was there again: "Butcher, Butcher, give me a dollar's worth. I can't eat all that." I cut off the same big piece and wrapped it up and gave it to her for a dollar. She comes back a couple of weeks later; she's sad. "I can't eat as much as I used to. Just give me 75 cents' worth." I cut off the same damn amount, and by this time everybody knows what I'm doing except the poor lady. She comes back another time and she's upset about her loss of appetite. And then I don't see her again. I think she died. I still have people who talk about it; we talk about these things that happen in the Market.

I am constantly working on ways to answer the needs of my customers. What else have the elderly got except food in their lives? If you're not healthy, you're not happy. If you're not eating, you're not happy. My thrill is to give something to the elderly that they can eat with satisfaction and without worry and it is blessed by me. Some of my greatest ideas I get from my customers. I listen to them; I care about them. Here comes a lady who for years has been buying and eating my ham. She's a robust, hardworking mother. She's getting a little older and all of a sudden she says, "Oh, Mr. Stumpf, I can't eat that. Give me this instead and please make it as lean as possible." So, I know that she's overweight, she may have a little heart problem. And then she'll ask, "Is it salty?" Then I **know** she has a heart problem. So I tell my customers what to do. It's just a matter of common sense. "I want real bland; have you got something without spices?" I look in their eyes and I can tell: **ulcers.** They trust me.

That's why I'm down at the Market, so I can learn what people want. Then I go back to the factory and tell my men what to do to make our product safe for these people. We are famous for our low-nitrite bacon. Now, our weiners only have ten parts per million of nitrite in them. When we make a beef weiner, we process them first because there is a residual of two or three pounds of meat in a stuffer that goes through into a new batch. So, I make sure that it's beef going into pork, not pork going into a beef weiner. I watch very carefully. When I say it's all beef, it has to be all beef.

I am constantly trying to bring down the nitrites. The thing about curing is that if you put it in the smokehouse and you don't put enough nitrite in there, it is liable to turn sour on you. But I know that if I just stick with trying, I can make it work. This is strictly confidential, but right now we are working on a big bologna that is very low in nitrites. I **thrill** when a batch comes out of the smokehouse.

There is a flurry of activity around Wendt's dairy stand. A troupe of Brownies in full uniform is lining up to taste the special buttermilk prepared from a family recipe. Gordon Wendt, the second generation owner, dispenses tiny Dixie cup samples from an old metal milk can fixed to the counter top. One little girl sits on the floor, puckering her mouth at the sour taste.

A polite and cheerful man, Gordon deftly quarries out pale gold bricks from the wall of sweet bulk butter, in the careful tradition that has kept the Wendt name a hallmark of quality for more than 80 years. Gordon's fierce devotion to his family's high standards has incited this otherwise mild man to joust with the windmills of modern technology.

The battleline is drawn over the burning question: what is a good egg? Federal law dictates the inspecting and grading of commercially sold eggs. To meet these standards through modern technology, gigantic conveyor belts have been designed to automatically carry countless eggs over lighted platforms for inspection. This government-approved process does not sit well with Gordon Wendt. He and his father before him have always CANDLED their eggs — an archaic but fool-proof method for confirming the health of an egg. He cannot be convinced that the mechanized procedure is trustworthy.

In an abandoned coalbin in the Markethouse sub-basement he has installed equipment to carry on with his egg-candling. A wood block serves as a work surface; a tubular can with a small hole in one end and a bulb in the other end is mounted on a bracket above it. As he rotates the egg in front of the funneled light he can peer inside the chamber and see if the egg is healthy. He is looking for blood spots, dark shadows; sick chickens continue laying but their eggs are contaminated.

Ask him why he undertakes this arduous procedure since the eggs have already been government-approved. He pauses, cradling an egg gently between his fingers and patiently explains: when the eggs are being screened on the giant conveyor belts, the quality control person might turn his head for a minute to talk to a co-worker; he might take a break to light up his cigarette. Oops! There go a dozen eggs right past him. He just feels better about offering eggs he has double-checked. When he says an egg is fresh — the customer can DRINK that egg! Anyway, he is used to doing things this way.

"Today, I think I'm the only one left in the Markethouse who still candles eggs. I won't say for sure, but I think I am . . ."

GORDON WENDT

HOW our family came to be in the butter, eggs and cheese business has to do with a strange thing that happened to my dad. He was a polisher and buffer in a casket works. All the fittings had to be polished and, of course, if it was a metal casket, the whole thing would have to be buffed up good. Doing the polishing and buffing, he lost his voice from all that dust. The doctor advised him that if he wanted his voice back he should get out of that work, quick — and get into something else. The doctor also told my dad to eat a lot of ice cream. Ice cream was the best thing to bring back his voice. So, he ate anywheres from a gallon to two gallons a day. This got him involved in ice cream.

My parents didn't have much money saved, maybe a couple hundred dollars. But, they had to do something real fast. Down at the bottom of the hill at the foot of West 73rd Street, they saw a little store. They decided to try their luck with setting up a delicatessen-type grocery store, and so, on two hundred dollars they started. Widemann and Company stocked them with inventory and trusted my parents to pay off their bills in time; they gave them their chance.

Little by little, my father's voice started to come back from eating all the ice cream. He was up to a whisper. People knew his voice had been gone and that it was coming back, and that made him quite a celebrity.

One day my mother happened to spot an ad in the paper about an opportunity in the Market and she figured that maybe that would be better for us than the little store. So they got a stand in the Old Pearl Street Market, and they were in that old wooden market five years while this Markethouse was building. When they came over here, the new Markethouse rules said each stand had to have a specialty. So my father, because of the ice cream, decided they would stick to the dairy products. The first group of merchants pulled numbers out of a hat to decide the location of their stands. The folks drew Stand A7 — and that's what it still is.

Those days, the parents were different than now, and kids had to work, that's all there was to it. I started coming to the Market with my dad when I was eight and a half years old. He didn't ask — he'd just come in and poke me: "C'mon, we're going to the Market." I came, but I had different interests and ambitions.

My main interest was printing; I loved printing. I was the only one at John Marshall High School in those days to do the complete set-up on the school paper, the **Interpreter.** I had a wonderful teacher out there by the name of Mr. Gaub and he and the principal pushed for a scholarship for me. I was awarded four years paid tuition at the school or college of my choice. But, my dad said, "I need you in the business." So, **forget** the scholarship! They didn't award too many full scholarships and Mr. Gaub was real put-out when my folks wouldn't let me have the opportunity. It bothered me very much, but when you were a son living with your folks in those days it just didn't make any difference what you wanted. So, here I am today. All told,

the Wendts have been in this business a little better than 80 years. Butter, eggs and cheese.

The eggs we carried were always the best. My dad and brother went out in the Amish country (they were **real** Amish people then, more so than they are now). They found a good Amish farmer out there and he used to bring them in eggs once a week. Years ago, the Amish never under any circumstances let a chicken off the ground. But now, with all the pollution and fallout, most of the Amish are feeding their chickens on wire screening like everyone else. Years ago, you'd get a chicken that was into an onion patch, boy-oh-boy, you couldn't eat those

eggs no-how! It goes right into the eggs.

Today, I think I'm the only one left in the Markethouse who still candles eggs. I won't say for sure, but I think I am.

During World War II butter got very short, like silk stockings and everything else. We had a connection with a butter factory and we visited them and arranged a direct setup right from the factory to our stand. During the War, we went through two tons a week. We were the only merchants in the city of Cleveland who were passing out one pound of butter per customer over the counter at regular serving hours. You can't imagine the mobs of people wanting that

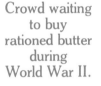

Crowd waiting to buy rationed butter during World War II.

butter. We hoped to sell a little something else along with the butter, but we were so jammed up we couldn't sell cheese or anything else; nobody could even see what we had to offer. We put up a few signs saying: BUTTER WITH PURCHASE OF OTHER MERCHANDISE. But the OPA man said that was a forced sale and he threatened to close us down if we didn't serve butter as a single purchase. Of course, **he** was always right in that line to buy his pound of butter every time we served.

We have always taken pride in our special Wendt buttermilk. Years ago, the brother and I figured out the formula to make a little different drink out of buttermilk, because it is so much on the sour side. We invented a formula to add a cream base to the buttermilk and my brother took out a patent on it. We had to find a place to process it. Miller's Gold Seal Dairy used to be over on 55th Street. We went over and sat in Mr. Miller's office and he offered us the privilege of coming into his dairy to prepare our formula. We'd mix it ourselves in the cooler; we walked through there as if we owned the place. We had our own cartons printed that we stored at the dairy. We would take a Thursday morning and go over there and bottle. It was all handwork. We filled up probably 500 or 600 quarts of our secret recipe every week. We packed them in wooden crates, loaded the crates in our truck and then hauled them back here to the Markethouse.

Today, I am still handling our buttermilk, though I've had to make other arrangements about having it mixed. I have some customers who say that my buttermilk keeps their stomachs in good shape. A few of them have had to cut down now because they can't have the cream, but occasionally they just **have** to have a drink of that buttermilk! They never miss the day when they walk in this Market that they won't have a drink of Wendt's buttermilk. It makes me feel kinda good.

Everything is big business now; you can't operate as a small businessman. These big suppliers of butter, cheese — most of them won't take any orders under 1,000 pounds. If they possibly could, they would put you out of business. The trucking companies won't deliver under 1,000 pounds. Our direct factory set-up man has sold out. Land 'O Lakes Company has been buying up all these independent butter factories. But, I'm still trying to hold my own. I've got an Amish Swiss cheese here that I make personal arrangements to get from two separate factories. I think it outdoes what anybody else is selling. I'm real proud of that cheese.

Lining up for rationed food items during World War II.

ANNA MAE GRADY

On a Friday or Saturday if you stop by Wendt's stand for a wedge of the special Amish cheese, you will be sure to catch a glimpse of Ma Grady behind the counter — the wispy gray-haired head bobbing up and down like a cork on choppy waters, the gossamer hair vanishing in a blink below the horizon of the high counter edge. Unseen, she scoops into the bog of large curd cottage cheese and suddenly re-surfaces near the far atoll of the cash register.

For over 40 years, Ma Grady was known as the Sauerkraut Lady; her stand was located across the main aisle on the opposite side of the Markethouse. A few years ago, when her children insisted that the one-person operation was too much for a woman in her seventies, she grudgingly sold out.

But retirement doesn't suit Anna Mae Grady. Depending on the season, she can be found in her home nearby sealing her jellies, painting the front porch, caulking the basement windows or pruning the trees. But when these chores are done, then what?

Ma Grady finds that she can't stay home from the Market; everyone counts on her being here. So now on Fridays and Saturdays she comes in to help Gordon Wendt in his cheese stand. When she first came back, the other merchants had a fit, each wanting her to work for him because she's such a drawing-card.

Call out to her; she will spin around, coming to a half stop to greet you by your first name. As she tilts her chin up, her metal-framed glasses catch the light, refracting off her blue glass earrings. Her spectacular dimple flashes with the hidden glee of a young girl as she confides that the earrings are hand-cut Bohemian antiques which belonged to her mother. She waggles her head, setting off a glittering shower of colored lights — like a crystal chandelier shaking off cobwebs. Since the first day she showed up here, a scared young widow with three small children to provide for, Ma Grady has inspired a special tender feeling in everyone in the Markethouse.

WHEN I entered training to become a nurse, they did not know at the hospital that I had only gone through the sixth grade. My mother cleaned doctors' offices and she used to have me come and help her sometimes. Once in a while when we were cleaning in Dr. Monighan's office, I would answer the telephone for him. He was so flabberghasted that I was so capable that he said to my mother, "She has no business helping you wash floors; she should go to the hospital to train as a nurse." And so it was Dr. Monighan that pushed me. He spoke to the superintendent of nurses at St. Vincent's Charity Hospital, Sister Francina. Sister just assumed that I was a high school graduate if I was working in Dr. Monighan's office.

World War I was on when I was going into my training. Bud Grady was one of the boys in the neighborhood and when he came home on furlough, I didn't have time for him. When you went into nurses' training in those days, you were on probation for three months and getting through that was my main concern, especially since I had to compete with all those high school kids. I couldn't be bothered with Bud. He came home again and asked if I was going to continue on with the hospital program. When I said yes, he re-enlisted in the Marines.

I didn't write him, but when he broke his leg and wrote from the hospital, I finally decided to answer him. He proposed through the mail and I accepted through the mail. Amongst my people (we are Czech) the young man has to ask the girl's father for her hand. I mentioned that to Bud when he was home on furlough. One day we were playing ball on the corner and my father was sitting under the lady cigar tree and he yelled to my father, "Hey, Mr. Macko, one of

these days I'm going to marry your daughter!" My father said, "Heck, what the hell do I care. Go ahead." Bud's face lit up — he'd done his asking! He was off the hook.

My mother and father said, "Oh, can't you marry one of our kind of boys . . ." Bud Grady was Irish, he was **definitely** Irish! In 1924, the sixteenth of July, I married him, and that was that. I stayed home and worked as a nurse while he finished 15 more months of service.

Bud Grady became a metallurgist's helper and when World War II broke out, the men in his plant had to work longer hours to fill the government orders. Bud had had to work on Thanksgiving Day, 1942, and now he had to work on Sunday. He was kinda mad because he couldn't spend time with the children over the holiday. He said to me, "I'm not as good as a farmer's horse! I have to work even on Sunday."

So, he went off to work on that Sunday. He parked his car under the Abbey Street bridge and as he ran across the street to where the men were holding open the factory's alarm door for him, he stumbled against the curb and fell on his knee. He said, "Gee, I can't get up." They took him straight from where he fell at the plant entrance to the hospital. And that was how he ended up scheduled for knee surgery on the next Tuesday.

He was up in the "white room" (that's what they called surgery) and they had his leg up in a stirrup. I could see him from the anteroom through the window. There are five or six doctors in the room and they are putting him under and I'm pacing back and forth in the corridor. And first thing I see, Dr. Jackson is ripping his mask off. And I open the door and I hear him saying, "To hell you say, to hell you say!" And the anesthesiologist says, "In fact, I'm not getting **any** pulse!" Five doctors in there and he died in front of them — that's the ironical part of it. They didn't even open the knee. He was 47 years old.

I had to decide what to do; I had to go to work. If I went back to nursing that would mean working 12-hour shifts and I couldn't do that with three young kids. What could I do? Now listen and see how ironical these things are, how destiny has these things fixed up for you.

Rose Resjska, the woman who lived in the corner house down the street, her husband Jimmy was sick, dying. They owned the sauerkraut stand in the Market and she had to run it when he got so sick. I used to go over to their house and take care of her husband while she was here at the Market. I'd give him his hypodermics and things like that. Prior to his death, he said to his wife, "That Mrs. Grady is so good to me. I wish when everything goes all wrong with me, I wish you would contact Mrs. Grady about the stand. I would feel better about it." He died in June of 1942 and Rose contacted me to ask if I would like to buy their stand.

Since the Market was only open four days a week and it was so nearby, I felt that I could take care of my children and work. In the mornings, I'd get them ready and we would all go out the door together. They would turn right to go off to school; I would turn left to come to the Market.

So, that's how I came to the West Side Market. I bought the sauerkraut stand and Rose stayed with me a month to get me started. Everybody knew that Bud Grady had just died so they were all helping, kind of getting me on my feet. In the Market, I wouldn't let anybody, but **anybody** call me "Anna Mae." It was always "Mrs. Grady." I was a young widow and I had three children and it had to be just so. Many, many years ago, my mother said, "Oh, Anna, Anna, you never should have been a girl. You should have been a boy." Because I have always been so cussedly independent. I'm not afraid to try. Now, nobody, but **nobody** in my house in 50 years has ever wallpapered a wall or a ceiling but me.

Well, there wasn't much to learn about the sauerkraut stand. You knew you had to get your price and you had to make at least ten cents on the dollar. So you had your sauerkraut, your dill pickles, your sweet pickles, your sweet mix, your jellies all laid out in big bowls in a pretty display. I managed it all by myself. My children would have to come and help me bring up stuff from the cooler. My Ginger was the oldest —she was 11 years old by the time Bud Grady died — and she had to take a streetcar down on a Saturday to help. That's why I say God was so very good to me; he gave me three good children.

New Year's was the big sauerkraut day, especially in '44 and '45, when a lot of Ukrainian people were coming over from Europe. They had sauerkraut for everything. One time for New Year's Eve I sold five barrels — 2,000 pounds of kraut — in one day! My kids' hands were froze white from the cold and wet in the barrels.

Ginger, Renee, Denny: they all had chores to do at home. When he was about 13 years old, Denny's job was taking care of the kitchen floor and the steps going down the basement. One time Joey Laitman and some other boys who played ball together came over. "Oh, DenEEEE! Oh, you got two sisters and you have to scrub the kitchen floor!" So, Denny said something to me. "Hey Ma, the kids are all razzing me about doing that . . ." I said, "Like who?" "Oh, Joey, and Jack and Ben." I said, "Well, okay, Denny, you don't have to do it. When I come home next Saturday, I'll do it." He looked at me a long time but he never said anything. And he never once ever said after that, "No, I won't do it." You see how things work out?

My Denny was going to graduate from West Tech High School in 1952 and he decided the sauerkraut stand would be too "sissy" a job for him. He came home from school one day in December, 1951, and he sat down at the kitchen table. He said, "Ma, do you think you could manage it so I could go to college?" I just thought I would go crazy, because I had never considered the possibility of college! I said, "Denny! you're not so good at spelling, you're not so good at math — why didn't you think about this **before!**"

I just made up my mind after he spoke to me to try and help him. The following day I called up and arranged to go see Mr. Tuck, who was the principal of the high school. I went into his office to tell him about Denny wanting to go to college. Mr. Tuck was a great big six-foot man and he had huge hands. He was sitting at his desk and I came in and told him what Denny said. I'll never forget the expression on his face. He put those **big** hands over his face, like that, and he said, "My **God,** Mrs. Grady! Why didn't I think of that? Why didn't I think of that?" He felt bad because Denny didn't have a father to guide him. He said, "Would you be able to swing it?" I said, "I'll try and if I get stuck, I'll sell the house if he wants to go."

Mr. Tuck made all the arrangements. He made the application and sent it in. It was through him that Denny went to college. His first year at college, he had nothing but "D's" because he wasn't prepared. But, by the second year, he started to blossom and he came out of it. When he graduated from college, he went straight into the Navy. He just grew and grew in the Navy, and they kept making him great offers, so he decided to make it his career. He has become a specialist in international political science, and he is invited to teach and lecture all over the world.

And there he is! My Denny's up for Admiral in the Navy. Mrs. Grady's boy.

Since Rita Graewe took over the sauerkraut stand, she has added a few of her own favorite German condiments to the display. The heady mingling of syrupy and sour fragrances envelop the stall in a voluptuous haze. A large blond woman, Rita's cheeks flush pink as she chortles her lovely accented greeting, "How are you, Lady!"

Rita grabs the customer by the wrist, towing her finger through the soft tar pit of prune lekvar. The woman retrieves her index finger, astonished to find it encased in a quarter pound of prune purée. Rita's abundant generosity keeps everyone frantically licking fingers.

"Yes, the sauerkraut is a lot of good remembering for me of my grandma, my momma."

RITA GRAEWE

FROM the time we came over from West Germany in 1952, I always did my shopping here at the West Side Market. All the European people came to get that good loaf of bread from Angie's Bakery. I asked the German woman at the stand if she needed any help. When I started working for Angie, I could not even speak English.

When Mrs. Grady wanted to sell her stand, I decided to try a business for myself and she sold to me. I still do mostly the same like Mrs. Grady did with the sauerkraut, the good pickles, the preserves. But I have now a lot of import stuff; I have more items.

I remember my grandmother made sauerkraut in Germany. She cleaned the floor real good. Cabbage, she shred it and then she threw salt on it. She bought me wooden shoes and I had to jump on it so the juice starts to come from the cabbage. After that she put it into a stone crock. Then it stays like that and Grandma put a nice cloth on the top with a big stone so the juice stays in there. We had it the whole winter in Germany. Yes, the sauerkraut is a lot of good remembering for me of my grandma, my momma.

People come from everywhere to buy my fruit preserves, they are so beautiful. Apricot and prune, that is the favorites. They say, "Pack it up good, these go to the airplane and I take it with me to California, to Florida." Sometimes the Florida people take the whole five-pound buckets. They're so hungry for Market food.

One time when the election day was coming, Congresslady Mary Rose Oakar, she came with Rosalyn Carter. She came behind my stand and she said, "Mrs. Carter, I want you to meet Rita, here. She grinds her own peanut butter." So she had a chance to see the peanut butter machine working. It's an old machine still from Mrs. Grady. Couple of times it broke down and I had to get it fixed because the new machines are not made so nice — they are all plastic.

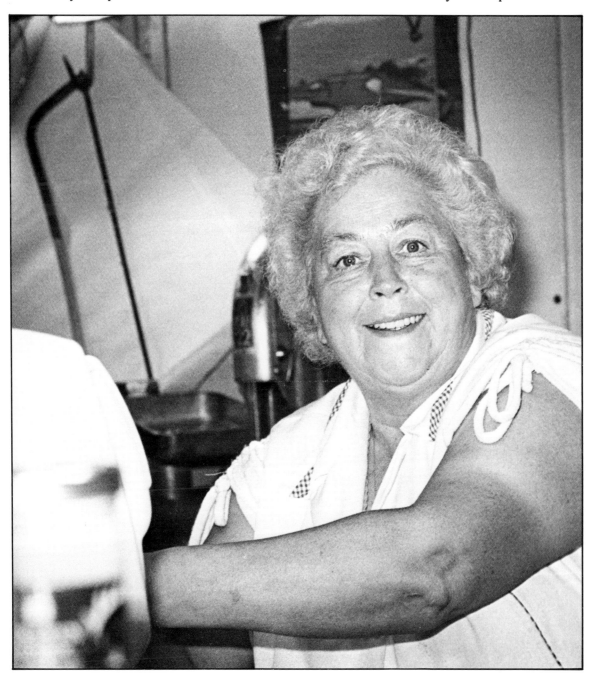

> **"Shopping bags is not a new item; it started in the early '30s. Prior to that people had baskets; we used to sell beautiful baskets for a dime."**

TONY LA NASA

Every market day a battered truck is parked in the cobblestone alleyway running between the Markethouse and the outdoor food arcade. Like a long-suffering pack mule trembling under its shifting load, the truck wheezes and waits for its owner, Tony the Bag Man. For over 50 years, Tony La Nasa, a small vigorous man, has been supplying the vendors in the Market with the paper goods and string they need to conduct their daily business.

His warehouse is just a step off Market Square Park in a street-level space that once housed a live poultry market. Tuesdays and Thursdays when the Market is closed, Tony is sure to be inside the garage-like facility, processing his inventories.

The entry is through a small service door beyond the old glass and wooden garage doors. The vast rooms are filled with bags stacked according to size, forming irregular brown paper stalagmites growing toward the high ceilings. The monochromatic interior emits the quiet aura of a Taoist monk's cave. The monk himself, Tony the Bag Man, performs his hypnotic ritual: slamming a load of bags on the big work table, slapping the bags to force out the air, counting the bags to fill the orders.

Like a true mystic, he prefers to be alone and makes it clear that any conversation will have to be accompanied by the unrelenting counterpoint: slam-slap-one, slam-slap-two. Tony pauses frequently to light up a cigarette, introducing a startling element of danger into the highly flammable paper grotto.

MY father came here, he was an immigrant from Italy. Let's face it, we're all immigrants, including the colored — except the Indians. This was Indian country and we stole it, we **confiscated** it — let's put it that way. We just run them out. We kept running them further west, so far as they got to the Pacific Ocean, then they couldn't go no more. And then we made reservations for them, after we defeated them in so many battles.

My father came here and he always had a stall in the outside Market, general fruits and vegetables. We used to come to Market with our horse and wagon across the old Central Viaduct, as fast as the horse could go, which depended on what weight load he was pulling. There used to be a horse auction on Woodland Avenue every year where we could buy a horse for five dollars and we kept a few horses in the barn behind our house. When we got to Market we used to unload the wagon and then we boarded the horse at a barn right over on Abbey Avenue and at night we'd go pick her up and go home.

We were five boys and my father had just one stall at the Market and as we were growing up we couldn't all live on that stall. There was somebody who was selling bags in the Market and his business was busted so I took over and started selling bags — big, small. At the time, I was 17 years old and my father had to sign for me. This is my fifty-first year in the bag business.

It's just an ordinary business; I'm the wholesale distributor and I warehouse everything here. I buy from the manufacturer and I sell to the merchants: grocery bags, butcher paper, string. The only place I supply is the merchants at the West Side Market and the Central Market; I have no other accounts. This is a one-man operation and when I need help, I

hire some part time. Whenever the Market is open for business I am over there, servicing my customers.

Originally my set-up was inside the Market itself. You know where the fish department is at the rear of the Markethouse? There's a little alcove with sinks where they wash up; I was right in there. The smell of the fish was something to get used to — it contaminated the bags and me! When they renovated the Markethouse, they forced me out and that's when I located across the street here. This used to be a chicken house where they sold live chickens; I believe the man who owned it was Jewish, a nice fella. This is where I warehouse everything and do my sorting.

The majority of this merchandise I have here is manufactured in Mobile, Alabama, by International Paper Company which is the biggest paper manufacturer in the world. They make so many different kinds of paper products I couldn't cover them all, nobody could. As a matter of fact, I've got a delivery coming now, which the weight is 42,000 pounds. I stock 14 or 15 different sizes of bags: number 2 through 6, 8, 10 — up to number 25.

On Tuesday and Thursday when the Market is closed I am over here from eight in the morning until four in the afternoon. What I do is I package a lot of merchandise. There are 250 bags in a bundle and what I'm doing now is I'm tearing them down to half bundles which consists of 125 because a lot of people don't want to buy a whole bale; I get a little more for the smaller quantity for the simple reason of the time I put into them.

Brown butcher paper is still available in rolls. It's a stronger sheet of paper, but it doesn't have an appeal. When you wrap a piece of red meat on a white sheet of paper — **that** has an appeal. At one time the brown paper was four cents a pound less than the white and when brown was 11 cents a pound and the white was 15 cents a pound, that was quite a difference. Not anymore.

Shopping bags is not a new item; it started in the early '30s. Prior to that people had baskets; we used to sell beautiful baskets for a dime. Today, if you could buy one for a dollar you'd be lucky. We sold the shopping bags 25 for 40 cents — that's less than two cents each. Well, at that time a nickel went quite a bit farther. Don't forget, at that time you could buy seven gallons of gasoline for one dollar. Cigarettes, we used to buy two packs for 23 cents, let's face it.

I have string, it's sold by the pound and it comes in two-and-a-half-pound balls. There's quite a few who still use it. See, when it comes to a big package, you put string on it. A small package, tape is fine. But a big bulky package, have you ever tried to tape it? Got to use string, maybe even rope.

For 51 years I have been in on every Market day. Even if I would retire, I would still go. Well, I've been trying to retire every year for the last five years, before winter comes. I don't know, what would I do? I wouldn't stay home. I'd get out of the house at least for a couple of hours even just to come down to the Market to shop. But just to sit at home and watch TV all day? NO.

Anyway, why should I retire? There's nothing wrong with work. Let me put it this way: work never killed anybody, but what really will kill you is **lack** of work. I can't just lay around, I'm not ready to die. I love my work.

Though many times I miss, I do go to church. When I go, I bow down and kneel and pray to God and I say, "God, give me **strength** — the rest I'll take care of myself." People go there, pray for money, for cars, for this and that. I just ask to give me the strength to **do** it! I don't want nothing else. You got the strength, you can overcome anything; you haven't got the strength, you can't do anything.

I like to be my own boss, there's no doubt about it. I couldn't work for somebody else. If I were working for somebody else, would I be talking to you now? If I want to go home at four o'clock, who's going to tell me no?

Since I am in the Market each and every day it's open, I do 99 per cent of my shopping there. I'm very particuar — I just don't have any taste for canned food whatsoever, for the simple reason I was brought up with fresh. Like yesterday, I says to Eddie, "I need some veal chops and a roast, about four, five pounds." When I got through with my deliveries he had it ready and I paid him and I took it home. I don't have to look at it, because I been shopping there all my life and he's not going to give me something that he knows I'm not going to use. See, there's nothing packaged in the Market; if that meat was packaged, they wouldn't draw any crowd.

I see certain people in the Market every day; I talk to a lot of them. "Tony the Bag Man" they call me but I don't know their names. I know the faces, names I don't know. Us older ones we have to find others in our age group to commune with. As you go by the hot dog stand on the way down to the bathrooms, there are always five or so different pairs talking to each other. Older people, mostly men, talking in whatever their native tongue. One day to the next, sometimes they're gone. Let's face it, they pass away.

We're not going to be here forever, but the Market **will** be here forever; only the faces will change. Eventually we all get old by living, so there will be others needing to be there. As my mother said to me, she said, "Son, if you want to live, you can't **stay young!**" As the young people mellow out, they're going to age like us, and they're going to keep the Market going.

HENRY PAWLOWSKI, JR.

Henry's Poultry Stand is located in the rear of the foodhall where much of the backstage action of the Markethouse takes place. From the end of the aisle a wide ramp slopes up to swinging doors that lead out to the loading docks. Cooler boys trundle dollies past Henry's stand, slamming shut the grinding metal jaws of the freight elevator on their way up and down to the coolers. In the corner next to the elevator the gargantuan floor scales shudder under the weight of crates of melons.

Ignoring it all, Henry Pawlowski stands over his work table with his back to the public. His large hands work expertly, boning a chicken breast, then scooping the excised shrapnel into the refuse barrel by his side — these hands that fondle wood in their leisure hours (his hobby is building poker tables and he has completed 25 of them).

The portly figure viewed from the rear belies a man who has endured three major back surgeries for disc removal. He admits that standing on his feet all day bothers him, but he shrugs: YOU LIVE WITH IT. Sure, he had to give up bowling, which he loved, so he took up the sport of pitching horseshoes. Last night he was awarded the trophy at the Horseshoes Banquet.

A passing vendor calls out to him; he dips his head in acknowledgement, never turning around. For a quiet man with his back to the thronging crowd, Henry Pawlowski nonetheless has been able to make some remarkable observations about his more than half-century in the Markethouse.

WHEN my father came over from Poland in 1908, he got himself a job with Fanner Manufacturing and he had that same job all of his life. For 43 years he worked as a molder; he used to wear longjohns under his workclothes and every summer night when he'd come home from work soaking wet, my mother would have a shot of whiskey and a beer waiting for him.

Neither of my parents could talk American-English very well, so they always lived where the Polish community was. Everything around them was Polish: the storekeeper, the church, the shoemaker. My father used to walk up to the corner to buy his newspaper, **The Polish News,** and he would sit down and read what had been in the American newspapers maybe a week before! He had to wait until the news got translated into Polish for him to know what was happening in the world. The first thing he would look for in the newspaper was the death notices. My mother would say to my father, "Look, see who died." My parents never had a car, they never went anyplace. Who knows, maybe they were better off in their own ways.

I'm going to be 65 years old and I've been in this Markethouse for maybe 55 years! How did I get here? I first came as a cooler boy, working on Saturdays. I was so doggone small I used to have to stand on the box to read the scales. I would get here at six in the morning, work until six at night. I got one dollar for that, and my carfare, which was 16 cents. You tell kids today about this, they think you're crazy.

I can remember people used to sell live chickens out on the square in front of the Markethouse. The coops were jammed full with live chickens and people picked their bird out of the coop and then they put it on the scale, feathers flying, wrapped a piece of newspaper around it, tied its feet together and put the chicken under their arm and went home on the streetcar. There's none of that left now; they all closed up.

Well, I had the opportunity to get this stand in the Market and here I am. In the early days we used to hang the chickens on hooks and the customer would pick out the chicken he wanted and I'd have to clean out the insides, cut off the feet and if he wanted it cut up, I'd have to cut it up.

Don't say "Thanksgiving" to me! That's a day I still dread. Turkeys used to be a once-a-year item — they just grew them for the holiday as a special treat. There was a type of turkey that came in already dressed from North Dakota; it was a process called "dry-packed." You won't believe this. They were dressed in advance and packed around in barrels with an open slot in the middle so they could air; they were at least four weeks old by the time we got them. They were just as dry as this piece of paper when you felt the skin on them.

Talking about how things used to be, there are certain tastes that are getting lost in this world. I'm Polish and there's a Polish meal called "Czarnina" which is duck's blood soup. It's almost impossible to get the duck's blood anymore. There's a duck farm down in Wooster, Ohio — Armstrong Ducks — and they used to send the blood in by the gallon. But the Health Department won't allow them to transport it anymore and the only way you can get it now is to buy the live duck and ask the man who kills it for you to drain the blood into a jar. You'd be surprised how many people ask for that blood. I say you have to be born and raised with that delicacy. It's a sweet soup, made with prunes. I like to eat it about three times a year, but if I eat it anymore than that . . .

Today, a goose is harder to get. Oh, you can still get them, but they're not as plentiful. They used to raise geese down in Texas and do you know what they used them for besides eating purposes? To weed the cotton fields. They'd take these geese out in the morning and each goose would start down between a row of cotton and just eat all the weeds.

Remember those sweet unformed egg yolks that came out of the laying hens? Leghorns are the best laying hens and it used to be that after they had done their job and were no good anymore, they'd kill them and those are the ones you get those small eggs out of. An undertaker friend of mine, his wife always made noodles, so I'd get a couple quarts of those sweet egg yolks for him and he would trade me fish for them. Then his wife would make real fine noodles, beautiful noodles out of them, and she'd always bring me a package down, but there's no more of that stuff because they don't kill those kind of chickens anymore.

The trouble today is all the poultry is mash fed, force-fed — that's the worst part of it. Years ago, the chickens would run around, eat the stuff off the ground. The older the chicken, the more flavor it's got. The ones we get in today are only 12 weeks old. The whole industry is based on a computer system which indicates down to a sixteenth of a cent how much it costs to produce chickens, and the computer says if you keep them any longer than 12 weeks you'll lose money.

Today, it's all production. The big feed company cooperatives own the poultry farms. They give the pullets to the farmer, the farmer raises them. They supply him with the feed, they guarantee him so much salary a year. When those little farmers were in business for themselves, they had to go with the fluctuation in the market. One week maybe they'd make money, the next week maybe they wouldn't make any — because the big guys undercut them on the prices. So the farmers decided they would do better just to work for the big guys.

After 12 weeks of life on the poultry farm, the chickens are shipped to the big processing plants and when I say **big,** would you believe some of these places kill and dress up to 70,000 chickens a day. It's all done on a conveyor. I went

In the
early days,
live poultry
stalls
filled the
Market Square.

to visit one of my suppliers, the Manbeck Company, in Fredericksburg, Pennsylvania, and I was allowed to watch the whole procedure.

The chickens are shipped in coops on flat-bed trucks. They take them out of the coops and hang them by their feet on conveyors. First, the chickens are stuck with a knife in the neck (this is done by hand), then they go through what they call a bleeding trough, where all the blood goes out of them. Then they go through what they call a rougher. Big fingers hit the chicken as it passes through hot water; this gets the bulk of the feathers off. Then the conveyor drops down onto drums with protruding rubber fingers and as the chickens rotate around these drums the fingers finish off the rest of the feathers. Then the chickens pass through what is called a singer — that burns off all the hairs. Then the chickens pass through what they call a slusher — a big vat that rocks like a cradle with slush ice in it. This cools the chickens off.

From this point, the plucked, singed, shampooed chicken passes on the conveyor belt into the dressing area. I never saw a cleaner place — all white tile, stainless steel. On each side of a 200-foot-long table there are women working, all doing different phases of "dressing" the chickens. There are about 100 women on each side of the line and on each side in the middle sits a state inspector. If anything isn't right, they just throw it out.

The dressing process involves the removal of the unwanted parts of the chicken; the organs and entrails are cut out as the chickens pass along the line. With a thing like a vacuum cleaner, women suck out the lungs and the odds and ends that are left inside the chickens. At the end of the line they have their own inspector and whatever he doesn't like he throws out. Then the chickens drop off automatically into vats according to different weights. They are packed in boxes and loaded onto refrigerated trucks. You wouldn't believe how fast the operation is.

That's not the end of the story. The feathers,

the entrails and the feet are sent to a dehydration plant. All these waste items are dried into a powder which is put back into the feed; it's supposed to be high protein. There's no waste in the chickens. So, the reason you can't find any chicken feet for making that rich soup is that they are recycled into the chickens. And, besides, there's an interstate law that says you can't transport chicken feet across state lines!

But I can still get a few chicken feet from Henry Schulte up the street on Lorain; he's the last of the old-timers who fresh-kills and dresses poultry. Tuesdays I go over to Schulte's and I take whatever feet I want. You'd never believe a guy that works like old Henry does. He stands there all day long and draws chickens, while his son sits on his duff in the office taking telephone orders. He says he can't sit down; he's been there too long.

This one old foreign lady — she just lost her husband — she's dealt with me ever since I opened. She buys two old soup chickens every weekend — she's the one that has gotta have the feet. I think she's Russian or Ukrainian or something like that. When she and her husband celebrated their fiftieth anniversary I didn't charge her for her chickens that week and I gave her husband a bottle of Canadian Club. Boy, she couldn't get over it. Now, she's the one that if you don't have feet for her, she doesn't want the chicken.

I never get tired of chicken because you can make it so darn many ways. Especially I love gizzards and rice, chicken and rice, chicken stew, chicken paprikash, roast chicken, cacciatore, chicken a la king. Now, I'm going to take a chicken home tomorrow — one of those old ones that I got from Schulte's — and we'll have soup and the feet, and then my wife will take the breast meat and bone it out and Friday we'll have chicken salad. Makes a good meal.

I'll tell you something. I've been in this Market so long, I'll never quit. As long as I can work, I'll be here rather than sitting home. I get enough of watching my retired neighbor do nothing, walking around in circles all day long. I come down here every day. If it was open on Sunday, I'd come in here on Sunday. There are always the customers to watch. They stand in the aisles talking for hours and hours. They meet, maybe they lived in the old country together. This is what is so fantastic about this place: just being here you learn about the human condition, but then you better be prepared to be **surprised** by some of what you learn.

For instance, there was the time that a little girl picked up one of those old fashioned money purses with the knob on top. Somebody had lost it and she turned it over to me. So, we got Al, the superintendent down here and we all looked in it and there was 780 dollars in the purse. By coincidence, there was a name in it and we got hold of the lady and she came right down. So, what happened? She left a dollar for the little girl! That has always stayed with me: 780 dollars in the purse and she gave the little girl one dollar.

This is a beautiful story. This little old lady who was a regular customer came in one day and she asked my assistant, "I'm short of money, can I charge it?" I said, "Yeah, she comes every week — go ahead." So, I didn't see the lady for about five years. She finally came back after about five years and she said, "You know, I owe you three eighty-five. Will you take a check for it?" I said, "Sure." So, I took the check and the check was no good — it bounced. So she got me for it.

Upstairs off the long Markethouse balcony is Commissioner Pilch's office. The opaque glass in his door makes it impossible to see if he is in there or not, but a slight tapping on the glass conjures up a large moving shadow behind the milky pane. When he pulls open the door, John Pilch is revealed in sharp outline: a tall, fair-skinned man, looking younger than his 60-some years, he is just slipping on his suit jacket and polishing his blue-tinted glasses, about to dash off to an appointment at City Hall.

On the wall of his office hangs a gallery of framed photographs that is a source of particular pride to him. Each photo features him in the center of a triumvirate with such visiting notables as the Pope, the President, the Astronaut. Under his regime, the Markethouse has been designated as a National Landmark and the clock tower has been carefully restored.

On the corner of his cluttered desk sits a large ceramic statue of an ape contemplating a human skull which he holds in his paw; the ape is incised DARWIN. John Pilch likes to ponder the small ironies of life as he traces with wry good humor his own unlikely evolution.

"When I came here as the Commissioner I said, 'Unbelievable! It's fantastic, it's like a dream.'"

JOHN C. PILCH

NO way did I envision it. July 17th, 1971, the first day that I was sent over here to take charge as Commissioner I sat down and I said, "GAD! After all these years, now I'm in charge!" I guess it was way back around 1927 when I'd worked here as a kid. Our neighbors had a vegetable stand and they took me along to trim celery, bunch carrots. You had to know how to trim celery nice because the outside leaf was soup celery and the other was eating celery. One was for poor folks, the other was for rich folks. When you trimmed the lettuce, you saved the outside leaves because a lot of people would come around and would want the trimmings for the chickens they were raising, or the pigeons or the rabbits they were raising.

At that time, a lot of people still used to do their own raising at home. When I was about four or five my parents used to raise chickens not only for the meat but for the eggs. And we raised rabbits. I was born in 1915 and in the early '20s I remember having my own rabbit to raise. One of those Belgian rabbits; they were big and had a lot of meat on them. That particular one you might say was my pet. I got so darned attached to it that I hand-fed it. The others that I had to feed I didn't get emotionally involved. All of a sudden, the day before Thanksgiving, my rabbit disappeared. I found out he was on a dinner table for Thanksgiving dinner. I haven't eaten rabbit since; that happened roughly 60 years ago! Here in the Market they feature wild rabbit, domestic rabbit — but I can't look at them.

When I came here as the Commissioner, I said, "Unbelievable! It's fantastic, it's like a dream." I hadn't dreamed about it, but if I had, it would have been a dream come true. You know, some of the facts of life I learned here as a kid maybe helped lead me back to the Market. My

Commissioner Pilch
escorting
presidential
candidate
Ronald Reagan
and Mrs. Reagan
through the
Markethouse.

dad always taught me: anything you learn any-where along the line, first, nobody can take that away from you; second, somewhere along the line you'll be able to use it.

For example, one big lesson I learned among the vegetable stands was: ALWAYS BE CAREFUL WHAT YOU'RE SAYING. I was able to speak English and Polish, which I got from my mother and dad, and out in the stalls I started learning a smattering of Italian. One day the boys I worked with mentioned that the Banana Man in the next stand was having his birthday. They told me it would be kind of nice if I would wish him "happy birthday" in Italian, so they taught me how to say it. I went over with a big smile on my face and I wished him "happy birthday" in Italian. He gave me one look and spun around — and from the hank of banana stalks he pulled out his huge curved banana knife. The minute he pulled that machete out, I knew somebody had set me up; I had said something **wrong**. I ran. He came after me and even though he was an old man he almost caught me. When I finally creeped back, the lady I worked for told me not to worry, that she had explained to him that I hadn't known what I was saying. She asked me who taught me those foul words. I told her, "Your son." You should have heard how she took off after him!

After that, she always reminded me that you have to be careful what you say, but also have to **know** what you're saying. From then on, if anybody told me to say something in Hungarian, German, Japanese, I checked it out first. You learn. You learn how to trim lettuce, celery — you learn how to get along with people.

I had worked in business and industry, then I went into politics. I ran twice for Cleveland City Council and got beat out by 300 votes each time. I thought to myself, well, I've got two strikes on me, I might as well go in and take that third strike. If I strike out, fine; I will at least have given it my best shot. The third try I won by 900 votes and I served on City Council for three

terms, six years. Then I got counted out. Soon after, I was appointed Commissioner of Weights and Measures of the Market.

Once you get the Market Fever you have to stay here because this place is so fantastic. Thousands of people come through here every week; we always have somebody new coming in. You can tell who's new by just looking out over the balcony. You'll see those people walking around, gaping up at the basket weave ceiling, which is a lost art form. That was finished in 1912 and we haven't had to do anything but clean it. The building was put up with good workmanship, good materials. The quarry tile floor is still original.

This place is a treasure that has to be protected. One of the things I had learned in industry was you have to have preventive maintenance; otherwise if you've got a little leak in the corner of the roof today, in six months you may have to replace the whole works. When I took over in 1971, right away I started fighting for more money to start repairing the little problems before they became major disasters.

The more people come down, the more the Market becomes known. We encourage the schools coming down. Some of them are using us as part of their classroom curriculum. The kids are coming down here to compare prices from one side of the Market to the other. In the supermarket they can only see the merchandise pre-packaged; here they are able to go over and see what a sheep's head or a lamb's head looks like. You know, as horrible as it looks — a tongue or a liver in one big chunk, or the whole fish — all become a learning experience. "Hey, this is food that we eat! These are the prices, we can compare them, we can watch the competition that goes on." There's no place else that they can go where they can find such a conglomeration of food.

The West Side Market is a municipal market; we rent the stands to the tenants. If you wanted to rent a stand you would have to come down here and fill out an application in person, which we would then put on file. There are 100 stands inside and 85 stands outside, but we only have 137 tenants because some people have double stands. If a stand becomes available and you are notified then you make your separate agreement with the party selling the stand for whatever fixtures, goodwill, scales, knives, what have you. We rent only the stands. As of now, inside the Market the stands are all rented. Outside the Market, we just rented the last stand this week.

In running the Market, I've got Al who is the Superintendent of the Market and I've got Frank who is the Supervisor of Weights and Measures. The three of us work as a team. In the event that any one of us is gone the place will still continue. If the three of us are gone, the crew knows enough that it will still continue to run. Maybe limping, but it will still go. What I've tried to teach is that you can't keep knowledge to yourself. You have to spread it. Nobody is indispensable. If I drop dead tomorrow, that doesn't mean they're going to close the West Side Market.

John Pilch
with his "right hand,"
Al Fiorelle,
Supervisor
of the Market.

A keen interest in the Schenck family's roots has nothing to do with genealogy — but much to do with gastronomy. Schenck horseradish roots brought fame to the family. The horseradish root, originating in Central Europe, was still coveted here as the essential condiment in the lives of Cleveland's early immigrants but the only place in town where it was dished out fresh was from the Schencks' curbside booth outside the Market. The father, an eccentric genius, had invented a contraption to grind the horseradish FRESH on the spot; customers waited patiently in line to receive the small measure of the pungent elixir that gave zest to their lives while guarding them against illness.

Everyone recalled the stand; few could recall the family name, calling the father simply the Horseradish Man. The next generation remembers his daughter Myrtle (who in turn grew old in the stand) as the Horseradish Lady. The three Schencks — Myrtle, her brothers Walter and Foster — now all in their 70s, are the children of the original Horseradish Man who set up his unique specialty business at the turn of the century. The Horseradish Lady's clear sparkling eyes testify to the lifetime benefits derived from the root's cleansing powers.

THE SCHENCK FAMILY

FOSTER: Our father was really restless; when we were young, back in the early 1900s, we moved 12 times in 13 years. He didn't get along with a boss of any kind any time at all. He said, "Those companies think they own you body, soul and britches." He didn't want to work for someone else, that was the whole idea.

WALTER: When he got interested in the horseradish business, he went to his father to borrow three hundred dollars to buy the stand in the old Pearl Street Market. Grandfather said, "Oh, you don't want to get in that business; that's a lady's job. Besides, you'll look like a monkey grinder."

MYRTLE: So Pa went to the Household Finance Company to borrow the three hundred dollars and they sent a man out to look at our furniture. That worried Ma.

FOSTER: Pa had his own ideas and nobody could change him. When he hit on the horseradish business he settled down and found his place in life. He saw the gold in that horseradish. For so many of the ethnic groups at that time, it just wasn't a meal without horseradish on the table. Those people thrived on it and Pa decided to specialize in just that product, year round.

MYRTLE: We would grind it **fresh,** right on the spot — that was the feature. But it is perishable unless it is put in vinegar. And, of course, once it evaporated you might as well eat straw.

WALTER: Pa was a very ingenious man and he designed the machine to grind the horseradish root. He made his own grater from a piece of tin and he punched out the holes with nails. He mounted the grater on a roller which would revolve by turning a big wheel by hand. It was a two-man operation: one person would hold the root up against the turning cylinder and the shredded root would drop into the wooden drawer below. You had to put plenty of force behind that wheel and we had a big boy, a tall six-footer, who hung onto that handle while he turned it as fast as he could. When the drawer got full, we'd slide in the empty drawer next to it. Pa dished it out while the boy did the grinding.

MYRTLE: Then the customer would buy a nickel's worth. We'd sell it by the measure, not by the weight. We'd measure it out in a whiskey glass, then put it into a paper bag.

WALTER: One time I grated off part of my finger right into the horseradish. I pulled my finger out to look at it and sure enough, the end was gone. The woman who was waiting for her horseradish saw it and walked away!

FOSTER: Pa first set up on the curb in front of Fries and Schuele; he hung his kerosene lantern on the lamp post in front of the department store and started in selling.

MYRTLE: We were out in the weather all the time, and we didn't mind it a bit. Horseradish as you grated it, threw off an aroma. Tears would flow and sometimes you couldn't take it — you had to turn your head to get fresh air.

WALTER: That's why we had the outside booth instead of grinding it in an enclosed room. Dad made the portable booth. It was like a privy or a phone booth, about six foot by four

Foster, Myrtle and Walter stand in cheerful testimony to the healthful properties of horseradish.

foot and we would carry it out every Market day and stand inside it to operate the machine.

MYRTLE: Easter was the big day of the year for horseradish; the ethnic people need the horseradish root for their baskets that they take to church for the priest's blessing. Russian Orthodox must have it red for the holiday so they added beets. The day before Easter, they would stand in line a whole block long, even in the rain, to get our horseradish. Sixteen barrels — what we'd usually sell in one week — we'd sell in that one day. That's a lot of work.

FOSTER: The roots came from Missouri. Roots are a big industry down south around St. Louis; there are farms for miles along the Mississippi River. It needs a lot of moisture and rich soil so you have to go down around a muddy river. You could get some locally, but they are smaller and hard to work with.

WALTER: My dad would buy a carload at a time. We would put them in refrigerated storage and then go and get three bags a week. We bought them in the fall — 100 or 200 burlap bags of 100 pounds each.

MYRTLE: You know, the roots would come with a little black soil stuck on them and you had to get that dirt off of them.

FOSTER: My dad built a little washing machine. Pa figured up an old cider barrel and put some attachments on, built an opening so he could fill his barrel half full with roots and pour water in there. He'd close it up and pull the lever which was attached to the belt and it would turn and run for about ten minutes. After that, the next step was —

MYRTLE: We sat, three or four of us, in a circle, and cleaned those roots. We called it "scraping;" we'd turn the knife, peeling it down as we'd go around. We got pretty artistic. Those roots had to be kept in moist bags, like a potato, to keep from turning dark.

WALTER: Another thing that really went over

big was grated coconut. The problem was how to get that hard shell off. Pa figured out a way to remove the shell without disturbing the meat. He set the coconut on a tree stump and with a little roofer's hatchet he chipped it away. After he got the outside shell off, he took a spoke shave and cleaned the inner shell off. He would drop the coconut meat in the machine and it would grate up just like the horseradish. So then we had a double machine.

MYRTLE: But horseradish was still the main item. We could always sell as much as we could grind. It's a healthful thing to eat; it clears congestion in the body. Sniff the horseradish and it goes right through. We never had a cold.

FOSTER: Did you ever hear of horseradish and honey? That's a very good cough syrup. You mix it together, half and half. The honey is soothing and the horseradish is penetrating. Oh boy!

WALTER: Some of our customers used to ask us for the **leaf** from the horseradish. They would put it in their shoes; they seemed to think it kept them from getting rheumatism.

MYRTLE: Pa created a horseradish relish: horseradish, mustard and sweet pickle. After several years we found out that somebody else tried to duplicate it, but they didn't have it quite right.

FOSTER: It was the amount of vinegar and the certain **kind** of vinegar. It had to be handled quickly and not allowed to settle and the fumes get out. You have to put the vinegar in the water, but you can't put the **water** in the vinegar! It's a certain thing to do with chemistry, just the way you can put vinegar in milk, but you can't put **milk** in vinegar without it curdling.

WALTER: Pa had the idea of putting his photograph on the label that we used on the jars. I thought it was a silly idea at first, but that was the finest advertising you could get.

MYRTLE: People would come to our stand and say, "Is this the place to find the horseradish with the man's picture on it? That's the kind I gotta get." You know, we couldn't go any place in town without people pointing at Pa and exclaiming, "Oh, there's the Horseradish Man!" I think everybody in Cleveland knew our Pa; he was sort of a celebrity.

WALTER: Ma ran the business after Pa died in 1941. That's when Myrtle quit her job at Western Union and came to help full time. By then the machine was converted to electric and it didn't take two people to run it.

MYRTLE: After Ma retired, I had the stand and my husband, Bert, helped. We used Pa's grinder until the day we quit, in December, 1956. It was getting tougher all the while after they had the plague in the horseradish fields and everything rotted out for a couple of years. Then, we were getting older and my husband had a good job so it wasn't necessary. We just said, "This is as far as we are going to go. . ." We sold until the last jar of relish was gone and then we closed and never went back. We just walked away and didn't go back.

In the early Market days, vendors set up temporary stalls along the Lorain Avenue curb.

Buying a homemade sausage is as intensely exciting as receiving a telegram filled with cryptic messages from a long-lost relative. The cultural Morse Code, spelled out in peppercorns and cloves, is eagerly deciphered by the recipient in the first ecstatic bite. This craving for the aroma, the dense flavor of the faraway place, spurs many people to the pursuit of a real sausage (the medium is the message).

The sausage maker who can successfully combine the homely ingredients into the desired delicacy is regarded as a true artist. Emery Lovaszy is such a man. Retired now, he spent his life as a sausage maker; for 40 years customers clamored around his stand at the Markethouse, vying for his products. One of Emery's great specialties was head cheese. The vulgar ingredients were so exquisitely combined by the artistic hand of Emery that people came from great distances to jostle each other and buy up whatever he produced. They gathered around his counter in admiration of a shimmering slice of head cheese. A peppercorn, a sliver of garlic, a speck of sage — each fixed in perfect suspension in the gelatin — looked like images in a beautiful stained glass window.

"I made three kinds of sausage: hot stuff, not hot, and some with blood."

EMERY LOVASZY

IF I was blindfolded, I could tell the difference right away between a Hungarian sausage or a German or Italian sausage. The Hungarian sausage uses a lot of garlic — that's what makes the difference.

I first had contact in the Market when I was 14; I used to help out on Saturdays in Szabo Brothers sausage and meat stand. That was my first job and my last job. I never went looking for any other kind of work. I learned to make sausages from Szabo's. In those days everything was measured by hand. I did it by taste more than anything — a handful of this, a pinch of that. By age 16 I was working full time for Szabo.

When I wanted to get married, my wife and I had to have our wedding on a Tuesday because I couldn't have a Saturday off. We went to Niagara Falls for just two days — I had to be back by Friday. It didn't seem right, me doing all the work and not even having an extra day off for my honeymoon. After a while my wife encouraged me to get my own stand. It was the Depression. Everybody was scared, stands were failing. It was hard to get established, but we had to try. To make the sausages I needed a shop. I rented a little garage-like place which was licensed and had some equipment like 150 gallon tanks to cook the rice in and some old stuffers.

My days were 18 hours but I couldn't afford anybody to help at that time so I had to be a one-man operation. I made the sausages in the kitchen and ran the stand in the Markethouse. In the beginning, I couldn't afford anything better than the hand-operated stuffers. The casing was attached to the funnel at the bottom of the grinder and you had to crank it to make the filling come through. I really ached from cranking that sausage machine.

Saturdays were the longest days, maybe 16 hours on my feet between the shop and stand. When I got home late on Saturday night I'd hurry up, quick shave and dress and then go out dancing at Springvale. Our crowd was about 12 couples and we'd dance every dance, changing partners. In our generation, dancing was our life. We don't dance anymore.

I made three kinds of sausage: hot stuff, not hot, and some with blood. With the blood it's got a different flavor. In the old days you cut the hogs only in the winter; they didn't have refrigeration so they smoked everything or cooked everything up. The ham and the shoulders they smoked, the bacon they smoked. And not to waste the other parts — tongues, odds and ends — they made head cheese out of all that. Head cheese was one of my specialties. It's the snoots, and ears — just a few ears, not too many ears — and tongues. You put it in salt for about a week and then you cook it all up in one big batch. So, after it's cooked good you take the grease off of it, cut it up in small pieces and then you put it into a pork stomach and add the juice, which is the gel

substance. You tie it up and then re-cook it so the stomach itself gets cooked. The stomach has a lot of fat on it; you have to cut it out and clean it, but it's got a flavor of its own. A lot of people used to love to eat tripe. Now young people don't like tripe; they say it looks terrible. After the head cheese got cooked the second time I would sell it in pieces or chunks or you can slice it. Some people came up from Columbus to buy them whole — two, three of them.

One good thing, the Markethouse wasn't open on Tuesdays and Thursdays so those two days I got up early in the morning and went over to my kitchen and made the fresh sausage. I did the smoking on Thursdays when I was there preparing the fresh sausage. I used hard wood for the smoking. You paired up the sausages and put them on a stick and smoked them over a day and a night. So, by Friday they were smoked and I sold them in the stand on Saturday. Smoked sausage goes well at Easter time. I used to go through thousands of pounds compared to 400 or 500 pounds in a normal week.

The rice sausage is called "hurka." It's got

pepper and salt and a little onion, cooked rice, liver, hearts. Years ago I used to use beef lungs and a little blood, too. I used to buy quite a few lungs and cut them up and cook them up along with some jowls for the fat content of it. Years and years we were using the same ingredients and all of a sudden they stopped us from using lungs altogether. I think it was because they were injecting the cattle with something that was getting into the lungs. Now they use them for dog food.

The sausage making was all hand work. As you stuffed them you would just twist them for whatever size you wanted. Yes, a lot of hand work. A lot of places haven't stayed with the same process, they've gotten clips where they clip the sausage together like a staple gun. Mine was all hand work. I used pork casings; they cleaned them at the slaughterhouses. But none of those companies wants to bother cleaning them now.

That's a big job and they'd just as soon throw it out. Plastic casings are coming in now. I think it affects the taste of the sausage because it was sure to get some taste from the stomach, but what is it getting from the plastic?

I ran my business for 40 years; you have to love it. Sometimes if I ran out at the stand I had to run to the shop and make more because some people came a long distance to buy my sausage and I couldn't let them down. I just loved the customers coming in, calling and gabbing. I had an aunt who used to have the restaurant in the back of the Markethouse. For years Aunt Susie ran the restaurant, serving good Hungarian style dinners. I used to go in there and have my meals all the time and enjoy seeing everyone. I have been retired nine years now. I had so much of it. I had so much work that I got tired. Tired of the work itself.

Steve Dohar carries on the Lovaszy sausage making tradition.

Steve Dohar
in the original
Lovaszy
sausage kitchen.

"If we went to a store and we didn't know how to pronounce the word right, it was a problem. But in the Market, it was like home." (Mrs. Eggimann)

All the fuss and preparation in the great Markethouse is to one purpose: to woo the customer. The Market without its customers would be like a symphony orchestra without its audience. Being a musician, Herman Eggimann is particularly sensitive to the fine ensemble playing and individual virtuousity of the vendors in the West Side Market, where he and Mrs. Eggimann have been faithful customers for 55 years. Although they now live at some distance from the Market, they have persevered in their sacred ritual of 'going to market.'

Stepping into the livingroom of their modest home is like entering a woodcarver's chalet in the Swiss Alps. The tall grandfather clock in the corner begins to chime; it is just one of the many masterpieces that Herman Eggimann has built completely by hand.

The fragile gentleman in his mid-eighties reaches down for the large accordion which is propped against the sofa upon which he is seated. Mr. Eggimann has another astonishing musical skill: he plays the giant Alpine horn. Haltingly, he leads the way down the steep steps to the basement where the ten-foot long hand carved Alpine horn waits, like a sleeping dragon. He hoists up the massive neck, inserts a special mouthpiece and blows the horn which has the power to transmit a clarion call from his house to his friends at the Market.

MR. AND MRS. HERMAN EGGIMANN

HERMAN: I was a pipe organ builder in Switzerland; I come from the French part of Bern, north of Neufchatel. An American tourist I met told me I could get good work at the Holtkamp Organ Company in Cleveland in America and he gave me the address. I wrote to them and they wrote back to me that I could come. I went to the library in Switzerland and got a book about Cleveland. I read the book and it didn't sound bad, but the book sounded nicer than the reality!

In 1927 I arrive here and went right away to the Holtkamp Company. I came in the office and I said, "I am Herman Eggimann from Switzerland." They didn't know me. Then the boss, Walter Holtkamp's father, came in and he remembered that he had written to me. He said, "We didn't expect you, but I'm glad you are here." He showed me the whole shop.

MRS.: The day Herman arrived, I was working upstairs in the organ shop and I was told to come down to the office — there is a young fellow from Switzerland and he doesn't know how to talk English. So, I came down and I greeted him in German. We shook hands and that was the beginning. I had come here by myself from Germany in 1923 and worked first in the knitting mill until I started in the organ shop in 1926. I made the little tiny pneumatics and valves and whatever goes inside the organ; I continued working for Holtkamp for 44 years until I retired in 1971.

HERMAN: At first, I was homesick and I wanted to go home — I couldn't stand it. But, she was working there; we married and after that I forgot about going home.

MRS.: Even before I was married I was in the habit of going to the West Side Market. I lived in a little rented apartment with my brother on Clark Avenue, and we would take our basket and walk all the way down to the Market to buy

our stuff. That was just a must. And the people were so nice and then I met German people; you could buy everything and talk your own language. If we went to a store and we didn't know how to pronounce the word right, it was a problem. But in the Market, it was like home.

HERMAN: We used to go always together. We were maybe four or five couples who would meet there, a reunion. We used to meet outside the Market and we'd talk about what was going on during the week. We loved to talk together. Now it is less.

MRS.: Old, we are all old now. We used to have our special spot. One friend would park here and one would park there and then we used to stand together and gab and gab. Then we used to go to Fries and Schuele Department Store and I tell you when they closed up I missed them. We used to stand in front of their elevator and let it go up and down while we had our visit. The drugstore and the dimestore; I knew all the girls

A rainy Saturday morning in the produce arcade.

in the dime store. It's not the same anymore.

HERMAN: Now, I cannot go to the Market, my wife goes alone. It is difficult for me to walk now, but I have my hobbies here. If you are a pipe organ builder, you have to be a real good cabinet maker — I make grandfather clocks, furniture. I play the pipe organ, the accordion. In the basement I have my Alpine horn. The Alpine horn is very difficult to play; in Switzerland we used it to announce the festivals. We didn't put it in the newspaper, we announced it on the horn from the mountain top; you could hear it up to ten miles off in the Alps.

MRS.: Up to this day, if I don't go to the Market, it's something missing. When I can't get anybody to take me in a car I go by bus. I walk up to the corner and the bus takes about 35 or 40 minutes and it brings me right to the back of the Market. All I have to do is walk across the street. Certain places I always go in the Market. I go by Meister to buy the butter — he's a young fellow. He's nice — even if he's busy he waits on me and then we talk a little bit. Then I go by Koch and buy the beef. He is waiting for me, he knows what I want. Then from Koch I go in the back to Stumpf for sausage and ham.

HERMAN: The Stumpf family I know from the beginning. The father was always a happy-go fella. I liked him; he was full of fun. We always bought from him.

MRS.: Outside we have the place where I buy the fruit, the Italian people know what we want. I got a woman where I buy my vegetables and my onions. I tell you, I wouldn't give the Market up. As long as I can walk, I go.

And if I don't come, they want to know where I am. Lots of times, they say, "I missed you." I wasn't there last Friday, but when I go this Friday, even the butter man will say, "What happened to you?"

Everybody tells me I'm foolish and nuts and crazy — but **I go to Market!** That is a **must!** I am expected there.

For 35 years Al Fiorelle has been Supervisor of the Market but he has never learned to take the place for granted. He is usually cruising along one of the Markethouse aisles, double-checking on a maintenance or repair job. Since he is usually just on the way to or from City Hall he finds it practical to keep his plaid hat and heavy jacket on all day. He shuttles back and forth, depositing the collected rents, handling matters with the City Properties Department.

Fiorelle means "little flower" in Italian and Al has developed his own hybrid of flower-power in appeasing disgruntled customers or in mediating tenants' disputes. His straight-forward common sense in handling the daily problems keeps the Markethouse scales nicely balanced.

"If a tenant passes away, we always contact the wife or the children to see if they want the stand."

AL FIORELLE

SOMETIMES it gets me down. The complaints. It's a public institution and we can't turn people away but there are a lot of petty complaints that come up that I have to handle. A woman came up to my office. She plops down a bag with three or four broken eggs, just the shells, and tells me that they were all cracked and running when she walked away from the stand last week. She bought them cracked because they were cheaper — she only paid 45 cents a dozen. But now she carried these smashed eggs back on the bus and she expected her money back. And she only brought back four out of the dozen. What happened to the other ones? No way the tenant would sell her eggs like that, runny, to go on the bus! I can't go down to a tenant and just say, "Give the money back." You have to protect both parties. But the tenant was good enough to return her money.

After all, our tenants take a lot of pride in how they run their businesses; they are handed down from generation to generation. If a tenant dies, according to the rule book the stand could revert back to the City and the Commissioner has the right to do what he wants with it. But we have never handled it that way. If a tenant passes away, we always contact the wife or the children to see if they want the stand. If not, **then** it refers back to the City. That has always been the policy here.

I have been the Supervisor of the Market since 1956; the West Side Market is the only City market now. I see that the rent is collected, I see that nobody gets short weighted. I have to check and see that the Market is clean, sanitary. I supervise 12, 14 Market personnel. It takes quite a team to run this place. We have three engineers around the clock. We go 24 hours a day, seven days a week. We have a day engineer and three at night. That's because we have perishable food and they have to check the coolers every two or three hours to make sure the freon system is operating properly. We have seven laborers and one foreman (Jesse), plus a chief engineer and three building station men who work at night.

All we're interested in is that the tenants run a good clean stand, obey the rules, pay the rent on time. We pull all the debris, clean the aisles and we scrub the Markethouse once a week on Thursdays. The vendors have to clean inside and in front of their stands. I check every night. I go inside the stands to see if they washed the glass and swept up. I don't have too much problems with it. Occasionally I might run across something wrong; I just yell at them or I write them a violation.

What makes this Market unique is that we keep it strictly a food establishment. The price is right for everybody's pocketbook. A lot of people don't realize that the fruits and vegetables are bought by grade; you can get anything you want here, from the most elegant to the most economical. This is a big place for food stamps. The merchants will buy tomatoes according to class and grade; of course you don't get top grade for what you pay for number three or number four.

People have cut down on their buying; they don't shop like they used to even two years ago. If they were buying three pounds of ground meat, they are buying a pound. Times are tough. Before, they would say, "Just give me that big potroast." Now they are buying only what they need. A lot of cheaper cuts they are buying now. A lot of them are going back to the old time ethnic foods that their parents used to cook: they are buying pigs' feet, tails and liver.

Oh yes, we have what we call the garbage pickers. Men, women will go through the piles of debris and pick out bad oranges and apples, peppers that are bruised that have been thrown out — wash them and trim them. And they will also go on the Darling truck. Darling and Com-

pany buys all the bones and suet from the butchers in the Market; they render these trimmings for soap. People will go on that truck and pick out bones and suet for soup and things like that. Myself, I would never touch it. Sometimes they will pick up garbage, put it in a clean bag and come up and say they bought it at one of the stands and demand their money back. I used to fall for that trick and I would argue with the tenants to give the money back. The longer I was here, the more I saw; then I realized they were garbage pickers.

But if somebody wants to earn a dollar, he can always pick up a job around the Market. The fruit and vegetable people hire a lot of the underprivileged kids in the neighborhood. They are being kept off the streets while they are trying to make a few pennies for themselves, for their parents. They also probably get some free produce at the end of the day. A lot of them grow up and stay here to work steady for somebody. I've seen kids come here when they were ten years old who are working a good job now. They have their own family, they turned out pretty good. Yes, I've seen two, three, four generations.

> "I was with my mother
> when she was on her deathbed.
> And, believe me, with
> her dying breath she said to me,
> 'Nate. . . never leave the West
> Side Market.' "

NATE ANSELMO

The heavy wooden plaque swinging from chains over Nate Anselmo's produce stand is more ornate than the signs of the other vendors. The letters carefully burned into the thick slab of wood read, ANSELMO, in a calligraphy as elegant as those incised on that other bastion of tradition, TIFFANY.

Anselmo's, like Tiffany's, is a family name standing for pride in quality down through the generations. Ignatius (Nate), the fourth generation owner of the fruit and vegetable stand, is the small, darkly handsome man working behind the counter. Like the floor manager at Tiffany's gently unlatching the locked jewelry case, Nate delicately lifts the lid on a basket of mushrooms to reveal the splendid white treasure laid out like enormous glowing opals. His specialty is mushrooms and sweetcorn, in season. His eyes light up as he launches into a lively lecture on the subtleties of coloration and texture, enthralling the most discriminating investor.

Both Tiffany's and Anselmo's command prime locations for their establishments — Tiffany's on upper Fifth Avenue, Anselmo's half way down the Market's outdoor arcade. But the somber huckstering methods of Tiffany's are not for Nate. A vivacious kidder, he can be heard, on a bright fall Saturday, singing out, "Step right up! We're givin' away the bananas!"

The youngest of eight children, Nate spent much of his early life sleeping on a shelf under the stand, which may account for his passionate sense of belonging here.

IT'S a race. That's what makes the Market great. This market place is more competitive than any place I know of, and it's because we are right next to our competition, within a hand's reach. If I reach out, I can touch my neighbor, and he is my competitor. In the market place you have to look at the merchandise, you have to look at the price, you have to compare. Most of all, you have to find the merchant who gives you what you want at the right price. He becomes your friend. Once you find a friend in your merchant, he knows you on sight, knows what you want. And he'll take care of you. After all, **repeat** is how he exists.

If you are in the Pick-n-Pay and you see thousands of items, there is no competition under that roof. You do not tend to leave that roof just to go buy one or two items at Fazio's a block away. The big supermarkets get to the point where they are no longer simply striving for money, they want power. While we are here worrying about **existing**, they are busy thinking about expanding!

So, why do we struggle to exist here? You'll find there's nothing like your freedom and the incentive to make it on your own. When you go to sleep at night, the nights are restful because you work hard. But, some days maybe you feel that it is a real pain getting up at three in the morning — those are the days when you say, "I don't need it, I don't want it. I'll go find a job with 15 paid holidays and three weeks' vacation a year and dental." And, if you really look at it, if you had a secure job in any sort of industry where it gives you all those benefits, you are better off. But somebody has to do what we're doing. We're a dying breed.

Our family has been here from the beginning of this Market; four generations we've been

here. My mother's family was always in the Market. My mother was seven or nine years old when they came over here from Sicily. As a child, she used to help my grandmother wheel a pushcart over the bridge to come over here and sell. When she married my father (my mother was 19 and he was 29), she had already spent a lifetime in the Market. She wanted to be here; she loved it. We have eight kids in the family —six boys and two girls. We all eventually went into the fruit and vegetable business and our lifeline has always been the West Side Market.

My father died when I was nine, but my mother would not give up the business. If it had

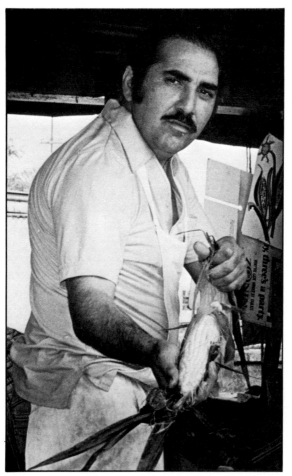

not been for her spirit I don't know if we would have continued on. During that very rough time, she had to worry about eight children and find a way to keep the business going. It was hard for a woman.

I was the youngest and a little spoiled, but I did go on the trucks with my brothers. We used to peddle produce from a truck, driving around Kinsman and East Cleveland. I used to hate it; I wanted to play ball and I wasn't alone in these wants. I had my brothers Ted, Gus, Tony, Joe and John. My sisters tried to run the house. It's not a story that differs from other families at that time. Six boys and two girls, trying to keep our family going. While the boys were out working, my sisters were home washing clothes for ten people, making a meal for ten people, and making sure the house was spotless because when my mother came home she ran her finger on the edge to see if there was dust. My mother was the type of person who didn't force anything on us. We felt by the love and warmth that she gave to us that we had to do it. Although we used to quarrel a lot among each other, there was a lot of love in the family. To this day, we may argue back and forth, but we're all together.

Before we had these permanent covered stalls, we used to set up our temporary stands all along the sides of Lorain Avenue. This Market was a hustling and bustling place — I mean it was jammed and spilling into the street. The thing I used to dread the most was the setting up and the taking down of the stand every time. That meant throwing boards across sawhorses, securing poles for awnings and tying the awnings down so the wind wouldn't carry them away. We had a big extension cord to plug from one stand to the other, so lights could hang over our produce for the wee hours of the morning and late at night. I almost got electrocuted one day when it was raining and the cord dropped into the water and I went to pick it up. Luckily, a friend of mine pulled the extension out of the lamp post. You can still see those plugs in the

106

lamp posts. I was the last vendor to leave the curb and move in here under the covered shelter.

My mother was really the root of it all. My brother John became the main link to carry on, but my mother had to drive him and push him, telling him to stay with this Market. She was constantly preaching to John that he must never give up the Market. She said, "When things are rough, you'll always have food and money; you won't have to worry. No matter how little there is that you have, you'll always have something."

My mother died about 20 years ago, just before I got married. She was only 61 years old. I think one of the reasons she died was just damn hard work; she just wore out. I was with my mother when she was on her deathbed. And, believe me, with her dying breath she said to me, "Nate, don't give up the Market . . . NEVER LEAVE THE WEST SIDE MARKET."

Speaking of how this place gets in your blood, my older brother is in the business and I have my nephew helping me and two other nephews just took over a stand, and my other brother is on the other side. Incidentally, I don't want to leave my wife out of this. She works for me night and day. She does book work, she does housework, she runs the business for me. Except for actually going to buy the produce and driving the truck — I think she does everything else.

But, now, who is going to carry on? You see, I don't mean to brag, but my son and my daughter are excellent students. My son is a straight "A" student in mathematics. My daughter wants to go into social work. Why should I force them to do something that they don't have their hearts into? We're here to live and do what's right for ourselves. I chose to go into this because maybe that's all I really knew. Now they have a chance to root out. For now, my youngest son doesn't want to hear about college. He loves the business: the produce, the people, the Market. The whole works. He loves it, but wait until he finds out how hard this life really is.

We need help to keep this market place.

Does the public want it? This is one of the last strongholds of family togetherness. We need help in bringing the younger generation here. Families are getting smaller, their needs are changing. Where they used to buy a bushel of apples, now they buy three apples.

Of course, we still have every kind of customer. We have doctors, lawyers, judges. We also have what we call the "late bus" people, those who come for all the bargains at the end of the Market day. They are people who can get an apple that is dented, a pineapple that is ripe. They are people who make use of their buys, they are people who know how to save money. But that's what's lacking today. I hate to say this, but the average person today does not know how to select a good fruit, a fine vegetable. If you tend to get bad stuff, it's because you don't know how to **look.**

An older person knows how to use the market place, to recognize values. Knowing how to shop is a skill that one generation teaches the next. Everything you know you learned from your parents, and how did you learn it? By being with them. But now there doesn't seem to be time for that togetherness.

The whole thing is that we have gotten away from family. Here, we are families still serving families; in our case, it's four generations. There still is a chance to save the old way. Don't put your grandmother in an old folks' home; bring her to the West Side Market! Take your grandmother out of the house; she can show you how to shop, how to save money. Those parents who raised you, you should be with them until their dying day. You've leaned on them all your lifetime, now they need someone to lean on while they tell you of the past. There shouldn't be any old folks' homes; bring them down here to the Market.

They have something important to teach you about how to survive in the market place. Our monument is here, this West Side Market; we don't have much more.

"Why, on a Saturday night it had the excitement of a frontier town all along what is now West 25th Street."

HOWARD SCHUELE

In the late 1800s the near-West Side was known as the "Haymarket" district. Blacksmiths' shops, feed and grain warehouses and saloons huddled around the primitive wooden markethouse. The Silver Dollar Cafe, with its barroom floor of inlaid silver coins, was an early and infamous landmark. Men crowding inside the Cafe were sometimes attracted by the ladies of the evening who beckoned to them from the balcony overhead.

In the midst of this free-wheeling frontier, the Fries and Schuele Company opened its doors in 1868 to offer the public an innovation — a modern department store. For 112 years the quality emporium remained in the same block adjacent to Market Square, undergoing interim expansions and renovations to serve a growing community.

Howard, the surviving Schuele son, presided over the family business until its recent closing. An impeccable and courtly gentleman, he is scrupulously careful to delineate that which is history from that which is hearsay in describing the pioneering spirit of those early days.

WE were founded in 1868; Fries and Schuele Company is very closely associated with the whole Market area. There was a Fries and Klein for a short time — Mr. Klein was killed in a hunting accident and my father became a partner. I have the original partnership agreements which were written out in longhand, dated 1879.

I was born on Jay Avenue, right around the corner from the Market and I can remember the old markethouse slightly. It was a one-story wooden building, a primitive affair with no modern conveniences. I do recall that at the end of Market Street were two blacksmiths' shops; horses would be brought right in there to be shod. They did quite a thriving business with all the vendors in the market who came by horse and wagon in those days.

Fries and Schuele was always a family set-up. I never thought about anything else but going into the business after college; it was just pre-determined. We had a full-service department store and also specialized in custom-made draperies and carpets. After we moved from the original wooden store up to the Ghering block, we remodeled several times and eventually took over the old Silver Dollar Cafe when we needed the space. We used the third floor dance hall for our workrooms and the balcony was turned into a lunchroom for our employees.

Fries and Schuele did a lot of special order work for the big freighters on the Great Lakes, furbishing the luxurious VIP quarters on the ore ships. It was quite the thing to entertain big tycoons on those freighters; we custom-made the draperies, linens, and fittings for the staterooms on board.

I think when the new Markethouse came in that really started the heyday, the growth of the

The original
Fries and Schuele
store,
circa 1868.

near-West Side. Our store certainly benefited from the attraction of the new Markethouse, which was known as a "good-cut" market. There is no question that it pulled in people from all over the City. Of course, when you say from "all over the City," it didn't extend out too far in those early days.

The West Side Market was a very grand place! Saturday night was a terrific night for business — we all stayed open until eleven at night. Why, on a Saturday night it had the excitement of a frontier town all along West 25th Street. There were fine boutiques, a fine jewelry store, fine shoe stores, restaurants, our department store, the Markethouse — all jammed with customers. I remember working in our store on a Saturday night, you just couldn't walk through the aisles for the crowds. While the women would go shopping all along the way, the men would head over to the Silver Dollar Cafe.

When the new Markethouse was built it featured the most modern facilities of the time for cold storage: underground ammonia-cooled lockers to keep the meat and produce. Cold storage was a big deal in those early days; not too many people had such a thing. We wanted

Christian Schuele, founder of the family department store dynasty.

to be able to offer a special service to our good customers: cold storage of their fine furs. So, we rented some of the unused cooler space down under the Markethouse and we were able to keep our customers' minks cool and safe in lockers right next to the sides of prime beef.

Giving up the family business two years ago was not easy. We had been offering continuous service to our customers for 112 years in the same location when we had to make the decision to close down Fries and Schuele. Up until the last day of our operation, our elevator operator was on duty, wearing her white glove.

Well, I'm 77 years old and I guess you could say I'm semi-retired. I still feel the pull to that neighborhood. I like to go down to the Market; it's like old home week for me. I plan to be there half an hour, and it ends up, I'm there three hours! I come home from the Market and say to my wife, "Mom, I've got **something** to tell you!"

Howard Schuele reminisces about his family's department store.

Early scenes
at the
West Side Market.

"When I look back on it I think
I should have rebelled a little bit
— I would have liked just to finish
high school ."
Lucy

CHARLES ROBERTO

What a big and beautiful family! Six sons and seven daughters, each meticulously brushed and ribboned. The powerful seated figure of the father looks out with unwavering eyes —calmly commanding the respect due a man who, through his personal ingenuity, achieved success in the market place. At one time or another, each of the 13 children of Gabriel Roberto (known as Charlie) has displayed his or her handsome profile from behind the counter in the West Side Market. Their stand has been known for nearly 80 years for its unique presentation of the best dried fruits, nuts, rare spices and precious condiments. The exotic cornucopia which has tantalized generations of discriminating shoppers has enriched generations of Robertos.

A closer look at this antique portrait inspires one to want to know more about these individuals caught in a moment of family pride. The litany of names of the many children is recited by Charles, the oldest brother, as he sits in his comfortable breakfast room. "Minnie, the oldest, is 84; the baby Victor who wasn't even born then, is 59 years old." As he tells about the remarkable Roberto clan, Charles is loudly encouraged and frequently corrected by his feisty sister, Lucy.

THERE would have been 14 of us; the first-born was dead. The oldest is my sister Minnie. Then comes Margaret, then comes Paul, then me, then Doctor Roberto (Dan), then comes Lucy Rose, next is Helen, then comes Anthony, Anna and then comes Nicky, then Gloria and Victor is last.

My dad came here from Italy in about 1892, coaxed by others who came before him. At first he sold hot dogs from a basket outside the theaters, then he worked as a blacksmith. He got into the Market through a friend, Marco Giuseppe, who induced him to open a stand like his — dried fruits and nuts. He was set up in front of the old wooden markethouse and when the new markethouse opened he was among the first to get a stand inside. He had the best there is: prunes, apricots, raisins, beans, rice.

I was nine years old when my dad had me as a runner, bringing out 15 pounds of beans, 25 pounds of rice, back and forth. I got so tired Saturday nights that I used to sleep under the stand and my oldest sister used to wake me up for the ride home in the wagon. I remember the noise of the horse's hooves going over the old wooden Abbey Street Bridge; a kerosene lamp swung from the wagon so people could see us coming. Kerosene lamps were used all through the old market; that's the only light there was.

I remember once we had a shortage of shelled walnuts and my dad made a good buy on 25 sacks of unshelled nuts from Italy. He got the family together after supper and we all sat around the round table cracking nuts until after one in the morning. We had to shell between 50 and 100 pounds of nuts so he could have them for business the next day. My dad took care of 13 of us and he looked out for a few others as well. Every Saturday when the Sisters of the Poor came to our stand with a little horse and wagon we would fill a whole basket with noodles and rice for them.

In those days the dried dates and figs came with sugar on the outside and I would have to "syrup" them. I'd put a little water on them, then stir to loosen them up to get the glaze back on them. That was my job every Tuesday and Thursday, which meant I never could go bicycle riding or find a little girl for myself.

But the girls were always waiting for **me**. I used to park my car in front of the Circle Theatre and every time I came out I had to use a baseball bat to get all the girls off me! When I was about 18, you should have seen the women who flocked to the stand when they knew I was working. I got a call once from Hollywood to be a stand-in for Rudolph Valentino, but I told them I had to help my father in the Market.

I was in the stand until I was 19 when I had the chance to go into the wholesale grocery business with one of the Lombardy brothers; my dad thought that would be a good future for me. I put in 27 years in the wholesale business at 80 hours a week before I retired, which is equivalent to 54 years of work!

Someone in our family has always run the stand; Nicky has had it now since after World War II, with the brothers and sisters helping. Nicky has the best there is — he sells fancy stuff

Charles, in knickers, stands next to his mother. Lucy, in a fancy hair bow, stands next to her father.

like mushrooms imported from Czechoslovakia that cost 80 dollars a pound and whole vanilla beans. I may not last to see it, but I hope my brothers continue the Roberto tradition. That's what our dad wanted. He told them right out, "It's the family, and everybody can make a living out of here." And they do make a very good living.

Nicky Roberto carries on the family tradition.

THE ROBERTO FAMILY:LUCY LOMBARDY

So, at the age of 16, I ran the stand. Because when Charles went into business with the Lombardy brother there was no one else old enough to come in with my father. I was in the tenth grade at Heights High, going into the eleventh, and I had to quit school. I had no choice, really, it was a living for the family. You never thought of hiring somebody in those days; the children had to help.

When I think back, I would have given anything to have had an education. My dad had ambitions for me because I always brought home good grades. They thought, "Oh, she's going to be a teacher." But then came the announcement that I had to go to Market. I gave them notice at school.

My brother Dan never had to go to Market. I mean, everybody catered to him, because he was going to be our **doctor.** Dan and my brother Paul are both college educated. I worked with my father and then, as they got old enough, I had help from Helen and Rose. Until Rose eloped at the age of 17 with the young fellow who had the stand outside. They were so in love and our parents were so totally against it — they felt there would never be a chance for their relationship — so they eloped. Their marriage has been a complete success.

So, I saved the stand for the family. When I look back on it I think I should have rebelled a little bit — I would have liked just to finish high school. To have graduated from high school, that would have been a big thing. But when my brother Charles had the chance to go into business my father said, "Son, that will be your future. The girls can sell in the stand until they are married."

My father had a lot of foresight. He had no education, but he was a very intelligent man. When he first came over, he said, "I'm going to go in business. In America, you're **nothing** if you don't go in business." My father had a lot of dreams. One of his dreams was to live in Cleveland Heights, which at that time was a place for millionaires. Oh yes, he built that 22-room mansion on Overlook Road and it was gorgeous. The third floor was a ballroom and it was all hand painted by an artist, all the ceilings. When we lived on Overlook there was a lot of prejudice. All our fancy neighbors were heart-broken because Italians had moved in. But it didn't really bother us; our family was so big that we didn't need any neighbors!

You know, 13 children in our family and we all had to be at the dining room table at night. Really, my father was awfully strict. I lived in that house until I got married. We had our wedding in that ballroom. My husband Frank Lombardy and I pretty much grew up together in the Market. The Lombardys and Robertos were like one big clan, all of us working in the Market in our family stands. His father and my father were godfathers to each other's children and two of us sisters married two of their brothers.

So, here I am, 75 years old and back helping at the Market. Nicky convinced me to help him in the stand part-time, so back to the Market I was — they don't have any retirement age! I have to give the credit to Nicky for building the stand up to what it is today. He has delicacies that nobody else in town carries. There are times when he can't get certain items, like when we had that trouble with Iran, we couldn't get pistachios. I think the hardest thing to get now is dried apricots. There's times when he can't get Brazil nuts.

Now I work two, three days, sometimes on holidays. And my sister Helen since she retired, she's helping. I said to Helen the other day, "For God's sake! When is Nicky going to leave us **alone?**" He says, "Are you coming in next Wednesday, next Saturday?" I say, "I don't even know if I'm gonna **be** here by then!" As long as I feel all right, though, I'm going to go.

Lucy Roberto Lombardy still helps out.

119

"I usually grab my lunch
downstairs in the aisles.
It's an inexpensive
gourmet feast,
and you make your own."

FRANK WEGLING

Frank Wegling, the Supervisor of Weights and Measures, is a handsome young man with a low-key style. Although his official domain is the entire City of Cleveland, his favorite province is here in his Markethouse headquarters. In weighing the important moments in his life thus far, Frank finds most have been held in balance by his relationship with the West Side Market, where he has felt at home since his earliest boyhood.

Along one wall of the office is a large glass display case featuring a beautiful old Gurley scales with its various weights. Originally used to verify weight, its exquisite mechanism could accurately weigh a postage stamp as well as a 50-pound parcel. Replaced now by digital devices, the scales, with its gleaming brass and bronze fittings counter-poised forever in their lost function, has taken on the aura of a museum artifact.

A lot of the things that I think I remember from my early childhood have been told to me, so they may not count as remembering. When the Second World War started, my parents emigrated from Hungary to Germany and they were in one of the refugee camps with a bunch of Hungarians. My older brother and I were born in that refugee camp in Germany. I guess it was a very primitive quarters; my mother used to dry our diapers by spreading them on her bed at night. People had to resort to raising their own chickens and cows to get enough to eat.

We came out in January of 1951; I was three years old. You had to be sponsored to come over here and my father went to work at the Ford Motor Company. A large number of his friends whom he had known in Hungary also came to Cleveland to work at Ford Motor. It was kind of tragic — people with doctorates, judges and provincial governors — they were older and really couldn't get back into it here because of the language barrier. They were all sweeping floors at the Ford Motor Company.

Both my parents worked — my mother worked at the Laub Baking Company — and they had to work different shifts in order to take care of my brother and me. It was kind of . . . uncomfortable. I guess people do that now, too.

We moved to this neighborhood when we first arrived and my mother always shopped at the West Side Market. I think one of my first memories of the Market involved a chicken I wanted my mother to buy. It was 29 cents a pound but I thought she said it was 29 cents for the whole chicken. I felt kind of silly after she explained it to me. That's my first impression of the Market; I was probably four or five years old.

I am 33 years old and the way I figure it,

I've probably spent 18 years of my life in and around the Markethouse. I went to grade school at St. Emerich's Hungarian Church; my father was the choir director. When I was a little kid, I used to serve at the morning mass at St. Emerich's and often after the services our first stop was the restaurant in the back of the Markethouse, for cocoa and breakfast. So, even in grade school years I used to come here regularly.

When I was sophomore in high school I worked here part time and on Saturdays. I worked for the Di Nunzios who owned the little grocery store in the front of the Markethouse. I really never had any higher hopes for myself in this place — it was just a good way to earn some money while I was going to school. Originally I was studying to be a veterinarian and then that kind of fell through. First, I was going to college nights and working at Crucible Steel during the day. I finally quit and went to work for Walter Simmelink so I could continue my night school. I was sort of a professional student; I changed majors a number of times. It took me a long time to get through school, working days and going to school at night. I went to Baldwin Wallace and finished there.

I must have worked for Walter for close to seven years, and I came directly from my job with him to being Supervisor of Weights and Measures. I guess you might say that Al Fiorelle, the Supervisor of the Market, was probably the person who made me aware of the possibility. He had known me for all my years of being associated with the Market and he influenced me to take the civil service exam and try for the position.

The primary function of the Division of Weights and Measures is to regulate and inspect all the businesses in the City of Cleveland proper that have anything to do with the determination of quantity. That includes supermarkets, grocery stores, pharmacies, factories, gasoline stations — anything you can think of that measures anything. Historically, the Weights and Measures supervisor has always taken an active hand in the supervision of the Market by virtue of his being stationed up here. It was part of my expected responsibilities.

I usually grab my lunch downstairs in the aisles — it's an inexpensive gourmet feast, and you make your own. It's convenient, simple, fast. My mother still comes regularly to buy her food. Since I'm usually here, I'm now the official shopper for most of my family. They call me, and on Fridays and Saturdays I walk around with ten lists I have to complete. So, that's probably one of the reasons my in-laws aren't coming around here as often as they used to. It's fun for me to go around and do all the shopping; after all, I've spent more than half my life here.

**"You get to know
who's going to aggravate you to
death; I just keep my back
turned and hope they walk away."**

ROSALIE REVAY

Rosalie the Cabbage Queen, like most royalty, feels a keen responsibility to set standards of behavior. She is highly sensitive to what she considers to be proper decorum for the give and take in the Market. True to her strong beliefs, Rosalie tries to set a good example through her own regal acts of "noblesse oblige" in her many gestures of grace and kindness towards the less fortunate who seek refuge in the Marketplace.

Because of her long reign (her family has had the same stand for 70 years) most everyone defers to her rulings on matters of protocol and any altercation between customer and vendor, vendor and vendor, customer and customer, may be settled by consulting Rosalie's Rules of Etiquette. Anyone deviating from those rules must be prepared to suffer the slings and arrows of her moral lecturing. Her message is loud and clear and any faithful Market-goer is sure to have passed through Rosalie Revay's short course in Market Manners: Touch, don't squeeze. Ask, don't yell.

WELL, I sell all kinds of cabbage, the green, the red, the curly. My father always sold cabbage; that was always our main item. If someone wants a head of cabbage he may buy it any place, but when they want a large amount for sauerkraut, for stuffed cabbage, they all come to me. A lot of my customers say, "Oh, here's our cabbage queen" because I sell the most cabbage in the Market.

My father was here 50 years. My mother and he were set up out on the street and as soon as the Market opened my father bought a stand in here. When he retired, my brother ran the stand for a while but then my husband and I decided to give it a try, which was 22 years ago. I figured this: my husband was on construction and they worked three months then they were off maybe the rest of the year. I figured with the stand we could always make a living. Maybe we wouldn't get rich, which we didn't, but we make a living.

I've kept the same stand, well, because it was my dad's. And I have kept the cabbage because he always said that no matter what else, you had to have cabbage on the stand. Even during the Depression, it was a staple; you could always afford a head of cabbage. I remember at that time it was two, three cents a pound; when it was five cents, that was high. Of course, rents weren't like they are now.

You have to have a certain cabbage to make good sauerkraut, and my customers know that I give them nothing but the best. If you make sauerkraut with new cabbage, it will turn to mush. You have to have the old, hard cabbage — the New York State cabbage. It's very solid and white. It's growing right now but after the first frost it will turn white as can be, then that's the best for sauerkraut. Between October

and November is the biggest month for cabbage when people make homemade sauerkraut. They buy five, six, ten cases of cabbage at a time. I really have nice customers; almost everybody brings me a jar, so I really have no need to make it myself. Some put caraway seed in, some put horseradish in to give it a little tang.

With the red cabbage people make sweet and sour cabbage and if they want to make cole slaw look pretty, they'll use a little red. We also have the curly cabbage, which is a lot easier to digest than the other; you don't get gas from it. I really don't know why, but cabbage kills some people, I'll tell you. The curly is really easy to digest.

Sometimes if it rains and rains just when

the cabbage is starting to grow it rots on the inside and there's nothing you can do. The head will still grow and then when you cut it, it's all black inside. I make sure never to give that out.

Oh, I love cabbage. I like stuffed; I don't like to make it but I like to eat it. I always put it in soup, or just boil it with a little bit of butter and seasonings. I'll tell you, it's delicious.

I have worked on the stand since I was 12, steady. I still love it. It's a little hard leaving the house when it's cold outside, but after you get here, put the awnings and tarps down, get the coal stove going — it's sort of cozy, really, and you don't mind the cold anymore. Of course, my stand is about the coldest because we are on the cross aisle and the wind really comes in sometimes. But once in a while we get a break and the wind blows the opposite way, so then my neighbor gets it.

I mean, we have a lot of fun, just us stand owners alone. If it's dead here, we kid back and forth among ourselves. I can be sitting home and I feel lousy, then I come to Market and I feel wonderful. At the end of the day, yes, I'm tired. But I rest and then I'm okay. Once you're at the Market you're always active. I stand on my feet all day, yet if I have to stand in line at the K-Mart that kills me. It doesn't bother me to stand behind my stand all day, but I just can't stand in line.

I sell an awful lot of avocados. Some people don't even know what an avocado is and they'll say, "What's that?" and put their finger through it. I have horseradish — nobody wants to carry it because it's so high, so therefore I keep it behind my garlic for people who are looking for it. You get to know who's going to aggravate you to death; I just keep my back turned and hope they walk away. For instance, someone will come up and see the horseradish. I have to sell it at two dollars a pound to make out. Some will say, "Well, it's really a little too high." I understand. They live on a budget. So, they're nice about it. But you'll get one who picks up the root and

says, "How much is this?" When I say it's two dollars a pound, they say, "Keep it!" and they drop it. Now that's being very nasty, therefore I have to tell them a thing or two. Like, "I didn't holler it to you. You stopped and asked me and I was good enough to tell you. If you don't want it, just leave it."

Across the aisle is my other stand and that's where I specialize in all sweet onions, greens. The woman you see over there is my daughter-in-law's mother. She's in her 70s but she enjoys herself when she comes down to work. She always donated her time to Stella Maris but they burned down and she told me she was going crazy staying home. I said, "Well, come on down." She loves it and she does marvelous. She says, "It's never cold here." She tells everyone that the Market's the best place in the nation.

My kids, if they get off work early on Saturday, they'll come down and they're all on the stand helping me. I have four boys and one is more beautiful than the other. There isn't a thing they wouldn't do for me. It's nice, it's family, you know. I had my granddaughter on the greens stand and she does marvelous, like she was raised here. My oldest son has three children and they come down. They say, "Grandma, don't ever sell your stand. When we get big, we want to come and work for you." I say okay. My kids are always dropping in on me. On Sunday mornings, after having a big day here, I put out a big meal. Come by my house at one o'clock, the kids are there. "Oh, Ma, you got up and cooked all this stuff." Well, I'm so used to cooking. There's always food on the table for them.

I do all my shopping here at the Market; I seldom go to the supermarket. When I do go, do you know what I go for? To be nosey. These people who come to the Market aggravate me to death when they say, "Oh, the chainstore is so much cheaper." But, it's not so. Like we got beautiful cooking onions, three pounds for a dollar. When I was at Pick-n-Pay, I looked at their onions: three pounds for a dollar thirty-nine, and they were **raunchy** looking!

There are all kinds of people who like to complain. I have a lot of customers who come every week and if you're a good customer, I'll remember you. You come back and say you had to throw a head of cabbage away, fine. You've got another head of cabbage or I'll give you your money back, whatever.

Then there are the types that give you a hard time. Like I had this fella who brought back a bag of spinach he said he had bought from me. He said when he got home it wasn't nice so he had put it in his garage and left it there. He brought it back to me in a plastic bag and it looked like green juice. I said, "Well, Mister, I don't remember you buying off me; you are **not** one of my customers. How do I know this is my spinach? I will not refund it. Look at my spinach — I have **beautiful** stuff." He said, "Well, I'm going to report you upstairs." I said, "I'll show you the way if you need help." So he came back downstairs with Frank from the Commissioner's office. Frankie said, "This man said that he bought this off of you." I said, "Frank, maybe he did and maybe he didn't. And if it wasn't nice he should have **refrigerated** it and brought it back to me. Would you accept this juice?" I held up the bag for him to see. I think the man had it in the juicer, that's what it looked like to me. I said, "And my word is as good as his. I will **not** give him his money back." Frank told the man, "Well she's got a point there."

I like to treat my customers right. Like my dad, when he put beans or whatever else on the scale, he'd get the bag weighed and then reach for an extra handful — that was for "good weight." So, a lot of times I give a lot of "good weight" out to my customers. Right now stuff is cheaper, I can give it out.

This is what hurts me. Last week I had this woman at my stand; she loves my garlic. I always have a few cloves that break off so I say, "Here." I always give it. Last week she came in

Backstage at the outdoor food stalls.

front of my stand and she stole a beautiful head of garlic and ran through the Market. It isn't the idea of the 25 cents, it's just I don't like people to take advantage of me.

I walked after her and she knew, she kept walking all the faster. I caught up to her and I said, "Did you want to pay for the garlic or would you like to give me the garlic back?" And she went in her bag and got it. I said, "Now, don't stop for any more free garlic because you don't have any more coming."

I have so many of these old people who come for a little head of cabbage or a little garlic or an onion. I tell them, "Don't steal and I'll give to you." They just need one onion. What am I going to charge them, they're so old. I figure, here! Have it. I give it in memory of my mother and my dad.

125

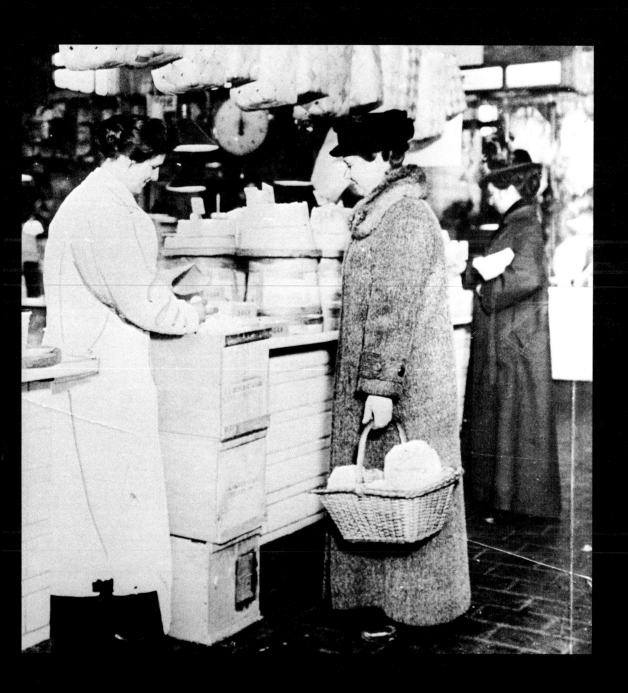

"If you get a fishy-smelling fish, it's an old fish, no matter what anyone says."

GEORGE MORONEY

A good businessman hooks into a rare opportunity the way a good fisherman snags a sunbathing bass: with quick thinking, quick acting. A businessman and a fisherman, George Moroney has owned the fresh fish concession in the Markethouse for the past 23 years. He had been in the real estate business until an unexpected turn in events led him to stop dealing with such problems as loan sharks and to begin dealing with man-eating sharks. Mr. Moroney is an easy-going, informal man who is bemused by his own adaptability. How he switched from selling habitats to selling halibuts is the story he likes to tell.

I was in the real estate business and I happened to sell a two-family house in Lakewood to the woman who owned the smoked fish stand in the Market. She said, "Well, now that you sold me a house, maybe you can sell my fish stand for me." I talked it over with my partner and we decided to buy it ourselves. And that's how I got started in the West Side Market way back in the '50s.

Frank Blasek and his wife, Emma, owned the fresh fish concession and he used to come around to my stand saying, "I'm going to sell my stand, are you interested?" I'd tell him yes. Then six months later he'd say, "I'm going to wait until after Lent." Well, this went on for three years. Finally it happened. When we went upstairs to the Commissioner's office to sign the papers for me to take over the stand, Emma cried like a baby. She didn't want to part with that stand — it was her whole life. After they retired Emma came back and worked for me for about ten years.

Emma mostly waited on customers and another fellow mostly cleaned the fish. Emma was there every minute so I didn't have much to worry about. I couldn't even tell a fresh fish from one that was stale, but I had Emma as my teacher. She'd say, "Can't you tell? Look at his eyes." I'd look at the eyes, and they left me cold. Good Lord, the first day I was working there I got my hand all ripped from those fins. She taught me to pick the fish up by the head. White bass, red snapper — boy, those fins are like needles.

When Emma and Frank owned the stand they worked out of an icebox. They paid the ice man to bring in 100-pound blocks of ice which he would split in half and set in the counters. They'd throw the fish on top and at night they had a man who took the fish out of the display

George Moroney's
assistant.

and put them in an old beat up ice chest and iced them down. I don't know how they ever operated that way. I now have six chest-type freezers and a walk-in cooler; we put in an ice machine that makes 1200 pounds of shaved ice a day. We've gotten in more types of fish and put in a bigger display. The thing just grew and grew. When we first took over in 1958 we were doing 500 dollars a week in business. Now the stand averages somewhere around 4,000 dollars a week. Instead of the original two helpers, there are four steady people plus the manager. It does real good. And the Market just never goes down; it keeps getting better and better all the time.

Our set-up is ideal today. It's a fast operation and we've got the best equipment — all stainless steel. We don't have to worry about health inspectors in our business because if you don't know how to take care of fish, you'll lose it. It's highly perishable. Fresh fish is odorless no matter what kind of fish it is. If you get a fishy-smelling fish, it's an old fish, no matter what anyone says.

Christmas time in the Market is fabulous. We get live eels in every Christmas from Boston. I'll never forget the first time we got them in. They come packed in ice and when you take them out, they're alive but they're in a dormant state. So, I took the eels and ice and everything that goes with eels and threw them in the big tank of water. When I went to take them out, the darn things were all awake and wriggling. I didn't want to look like I was afraid of them with Emma there. So, I dug in and threw some onto the counter. And, God! They were squirming and traveling all through the showcase and these Italian women were buying them like crazy. They thought it was tremendous. I guess it's just a Christmas custom with Italian people.

Another thing we used to do — and still do every Christmas — is go up and get a whole truckload of live carp at Cold Creek, Ohio. The fellow out there has pens that go down into the Blue Hole, so it never freezes in the wintertime.

You can see the pens from Lake Road, this side of Sandusky bridge. I back my truck in there and these guys go down and get great big scoops of live carp out of the water. I get back with 4,000 pounds, as much as the truck will hold; I haul them back and sell them all Christmas week. You prepare for six months, getting everything together for Christmas in the Market.

We used to sell a lot of fish called "lutefisk," which the Swedes eat for Christmas. They take dried cod, which is as hard as the table, and they soak it in lye water and the stuff blooms back up to its original size. Then they put it through seven rinse waters. We get it in and it's like a big piece of blubber. We've got to wrap it in waxed paper because it's so wet and floppy.

We have sold everything in there that walked or swam in the oceans. We sold live turtles. We still do when we can get them. They come from Canada. These are snapping turtles and they'll break your pencil in half if they can get it in their mouths. They'd come in burlap bags and I stored them that way in the cooler to keep them quiet. Then we'd flood one of the showcases and put a couple in there for show. They'd get pretty friendly to the point where I could feed them smelts and they wouldn't snap at me. Then I got attached to the darn things so I had to cut that out. They were nice. Anybody that knows turtles knows they're delicious — turtle soup, turtle steaks. Well, all we did was cut the head off, give it to the customer like that.

We sell shark whenever we can get it; it sells real good. Maco shark, that's the one that's the man-eater. We get a chunk of it or sometimes we buy the whole shark, maybe one that weighs 135 pounds. We used to handle sea urchins but they're not available anymore. You scrape off the bristles, bust into it and it's like yellow liquid inside. Some people eat it right out of the shell without cooking it or anything. I tasted it once — Oh, God!

I'll tell you something about skates. We get them down at the Market and everybody wants them skinned because one side is dark with burrs on it and you could cut your fingers. The other side is white and smooth. Back during World War II scallops were in short supply and disreputable fishermen would take the skates and with a special cutter they would knock out chunks of skate the size and shape of scallops. They were selling the skates for scallops and nobody knew it.

We get king salmon and silver salmon comes in frozen from Alaska or the state of Washington. Every Monday morning I call Emory in Virginia, then we call Detroit, Michigan, and talk to an outfit there. Those are our main suppliers. Fresh tuna is expensive now because of competition with the Japanese. They buy all the tuna that comes out of Boston and they pay the price. The price is prohibitive.

There are two things that have really helped our business. One is the high price of beef and pork; many people now are making a main meal with fish. And people are more aware of their health. There's a lot of talk about getting your protein; fish is rich in protein. So, it can't but help the business. We give 50 pounds of fish a week to the Hunger Task Force over at St. Phillip's Church. I figured there's no better food that you can give than fish. Oh, gosh, they're crazy for it. I wish I could give them more, but I give them a full box of fish every week.

We get people regularly from places like Lorain, Akron and Youngstown — everywhere in Ohio because we're the only place that has such a choice of fish. And the people come from out of state, from everywhere. The only thing is, though, when the big politicians make their swing through the Market they don't remember to come through our fish department. Once, when Nixon was coming through, I put up a big sign across our entrance, "Here's to our next President, Richard Nixon." I mean I didn't **vote** for him, but I hoped he'd see the sign from out there and come walking through, but he never did.

I own the stand, but now I'm leaving the responsibility of running it mainly to my manager, Ilyia. I was in various stages of retirement and finally, ten months ago, I retired. So far, I love it. Now I can go fishing two, maybe three times a week. I like to get alongside a river and just throw my line out.

WALTER F. SIMMELINK, JR.

On Tuesdays and Thursdays when the Market is closed to the public, a different kind of activity can be observed: along the back docks, tractor-trailers and family vans vie for position, unloading everything from sides of beef to baskets of homegrown mushrooms. Metal wheeled dollies squeak back and forth to the freight elevators, carrying the produce down into the coolers for storage.

Inside the darkened Markethouse, huge scrubbing machines labor up and down the aisles, whirring clean the red quarry tiles. It is difficult to locate the maintenance crews in the semi-darkness; a few years ago the splendid glass transoms crowning either end of the foodhall were covered over with painted metal murals, robbing the place of natural light (the windows were deemed to be too much trouble to clean).

Within this somber cavern there is a flicker of light along the far wall; a glaring spotlight in the otherwise blackened theatre focuses on a solitary figure. He is cast in a pool of harsh light. Like an actor blocking out his soliloquy on an empty stage, Walter Simmelink moves gracefully back and forth beneath the glint of his counter light. Simmelink's cheese and dairy stand has occupied that same place along the wall since Day One, 1912. In the dimness it would be easy to mistake Walter, Jr., for his father before him.

This elegant, soft-spoken gentleman is likely to be here in the Markethouse on off-days and at off-hours. As he peers over his glasses to read the scales he looks more like a foreign diplomat deciphering a cablegram than a merchant weighing a chunk of cheddar.

Walter is an acknowledged authority when it comes to gourmet cheeses, and "afficionados" flock from great distances to come and discuss with him the idiosyncracies of Gorgonzola and Gruyère.

MY father's family came from Holland in the early 1880s and Grandfather Simmelink had a job in an industrial plant down in Cleveland's Flats. He would walk to work, and walk home from work, and he would sew the family's shoes and cut the family's hair. He lived to be a ripe 88 years old. My grandparents were so religious that a Sunday paper was not permitted in their home.

My father would have been a great professional man had not his older brother died, making it necessary for him to help support the family as soon as he finished high school. He had taken four years of Latin, three years of Greek, and he was an accomplished musician. He maintained his musical interest throughout his lifetime and played the organ for 25 years at the Calvary Reformed Church. If I have any hobbies, to this day I love to listen to organ music.

Father had been working for a vendor in the Pearl Street Market but on a cold winter day in 1911, after his request for a raise had been refused, he decided to go out on his own. So, at the tender age of 23, my father was able to buy his own stand for a very reasonable price because business was poor on that wintry day. The next year, when the new Markethouse opened, he had third choice in the drawing for locations; Simmelink's has had the same stand since 1912.

From the beginning my father pioneered in merchandising methods, venturing to New York, to Chicago, to buy cheeses at the right price. He spent money to make money. Establishing out-of-city contacts was unusual in those early days, but that broad base of suppliers helped propel him beyond some of the less adventurous local merchants.

He soon banded together with a group of

progressive merchants to form the West Side Market Tenants' Association. Originally organized to promote the new Markethouse and to lobby for tenants' requirements, the Association has grown over the years and has been instrumental in bringing about important improvements in the Markethouse. For instance, in the 1954 renovation, those windows up near the ceiling were all bricked in. There was no way for the hot air to escape and the heat in here was intense in the summer. A request for an installation of window fans was refused because the remodeling job had just been completed. The Association went directly to City Hall and within six months the city paid $25,000 to have those exhaust fans installed. So I say the strength of the Markethouse is in the strength of the Association. I myself have been on the Board of Directors for 36 years; I've served as president for eight years and right now I'm secretary. I'm a

little bit proud of helping to maintain that special tradition.

I grew up in the cheese business and when I began to consider it as a career, my father encouraged me to get the best technical education possible. In my second year at Iowa State University, I won first prize in cheese making and in my third year I won first prize in butter making — and that's not too bad for a city kid! When I graduated with a bachelor of science degree in dairy technology, I found that I had a tremendous advantage in running the business; I began to attract a discriminating clientele who came to rely on my special knowledge.

Today, the connoisseur prefers the natural cheeses which are self-curing; the older they get, the riper they get. There are certain stages that some people really fancy. Through my study of fermentation and bacterial changes I know how most basic cheeses are formulated and I know just when to pluck them. I look at a few brie cheeses when they come in and I have a pretty good idea as to their maturity. If they come in a bit young, I force them a little by putting them in a warm room.

Through my reputation, I've become acquainted with some of the world's finest people; Maestro Lorin Maazel buys his cheese here. When the King of Saudi Arabia was at the

The world of Walter Simmelink, encapsulated here.

134

Cleveland Clinic for heart surgery, his entourage was sent to me for his cheeses. Your better cheese still comes from Europe where the art is handed down from generation to generation; it takes a lot of pains and care to make a pound of cheese. In this country, everybody tastes the dollar bill. In making Swiss cheese here they turn it out in six weeks, whereas in Switzerland they will not sell a cheese until it is at least 100 days old.

In keeping with our origins, the original Holland Edam, looking like a four-pound cannon ball, is still very close to us and we have a Leyden spiced cheese with caraway and cumin seeds that is well known to the Dutch people.

I am very proud of the large wholesale operation I've developed over the years. I am the distributor to most of the fine hotels, restaurants and country clubs in this area and I run the whole enterprise right out of this stand! It's unbelievable the amount of business we are doing from this small physical set-up. I oversee everything myself with the aid of a 24-hour answering service to keep in touch with our numerous accounts.

I hold import licenses that give me exclusive distribution rights on certain cheeses from Australia and New Zealand which move directly off the pier in New York without my ever seeing them. Tomorrow I'll be out on the loading dock here waiting to take delivery on a 9,000-pound order.

With all the demands of my wholesale distributing operation, I've been asked why I keep this stand. I think it comes down to the basic loving to serve people. A person stands in front of my counter and has a few moments of chit-chat; maybe I'm the only person he or she will come in contact with all day. That's one of the things that holds me to the Market. I think at times we are all a little bit lonely; it's awful to be lonely. Isn't it nice to come here and be greeted by your favorite merchant, whether or not you want to buy anything.

"In that stand
there were three fellows
all cutting meat left-handed.
That's one for Ripley."

WILLIS BAUMGARDNER

Visitors to the Markethouse often exclaim over the structure's excellent condition; after 70 years it shows remarkably little wear and tear. They might also exclaim over Willis Baumgardner who, at 81, bears even fewer scuff marks than the sturdy building. Although he has promised to retire many times, he still helps out two days a week in a meat stand, maintaining his record as the oldest butcher working here.

In his leisure time, Willis loves to play golf. His vigorous stance on the fairway may result from his lifetime of standing astride the butcher block. The steady swing relies on a strong arm still conditioned by hand-cutting meat. Although he has yet to set any records on the golf course, he grins mischievously as he takes clean swipes at the ball and neatly slices up the green.

I was born in 1900, so I'm always the same age as the century; that makes me 81 years old. We lived off of West 26th Street, just a block away from the Market and of course I'd tag along with my mother when she went shopping, help her carry the bag. I was 13 going on 14 when old Eddie Weigel said, "How about a job sometime?" That was how I got started in the butcher business — it was November, 1914, 67 years ago.

I got involved in washing the tools and scrubbing the blocks and sweeping out. Gradually you pick things up. In those early days everything was cut upstairs, all cut by hand. In Weigel's stand there were two butchers; Ed Weigel cut left-handed and Alvin Zerby cut left-handed. I am right-handed. Well, you follow the man who's teaching you. I converted to left-handed. So, in that little stand there were three fellows all cutting meat left-handed. That's one for Ripley. These aren't meat cutters nowadays with electric tools; these are "saw jockeys."

Eventually I got my own stand in the Markethouse. At that time there was no refrigeration upstairs so I rigged up a little invention. My neighbor got me two sheets of stainless steel cut to fit the whole one side of the counter and I had a tank built. I would fill it with dry ice and that would give me refrigeration and it lasted quite a while. I attached a blower, but that was too much; it dried out the meat and changed the color to grey. I still had that ice tank up until they put in the new counters in 1953.

Competition, we had a lot of that. But I always said the only thing that counts is when you ring your own register. That's how you make your money, when you're ringing **your** register, not your neighbor's. You worked until you were **through**, until you were sold out.

I had sold my stand quite a while ago and tried my hand at a few other businesses over the years. A little over a year ago, I got sick. The doctor said he wouldn't put me in the hospital if I promised to stay home for ten days. So, I'd rather stay home than go to the hospital; I stayed home for about two weeks. When I was feeling better I went down to the Markethouse and I was taking a walk around. I got as far as Chuck when he said to me, "Willis, are you working?" I told him no, I wasn't and he asked me if I would like to work Fridays and Saturdays for him. He said, "Do you want to start next week?" That was a year ago September and I've been back here working as a butcher ever since.

It's in your blood, it's something you've done, you're interested in it. Let me put it this way: when Thursday comes around I get a little excited and I will say to Peg, "I gotta go to work tomorrow." I love those two days.

Willis Baumgardner,
in the early days,
behind his stand.

High in the Andes Mountains of Peru and Bolivia, where the potato has been a staple for thousands of years, legend says that it was a gift of the gods; they gave the Indians seed that produced beautiful plants. The invading enemies ate these seductive plants and became sick. Then the gods instructed the Indians to shun the plants but eat the roots; they grew strong and vanquished the invaders.

From that time on, the potato, hiding its blemished head under the ground, could no longer conceal its magic powers. The rest of the world began to learn of "potato power" in the sixteenth century, when the Spaniards carried home some of the starchy nuggets. Their value came to outweigh all the gold plundered from the Incas.

By the end of the eighteenth century, potatoes were the major crop in continental Europe, and Ireland embraced them as the elixir of its life. Because production of this food from a small plot of ground could feed a family and yield a surplus to sell, the potato helped to make possible the Industrial Revolution. But the blight that led to the Irish Potato Famine in the 1840s unleashed the tragedy implicit in that passionate relationship.

Today, medical researchers have found that the root that made the Incas strong may be the antidote for malnutrition. Starving children lose the capacity to digest milk; potatoes serve as a replacement, providing the needed high-quality protein. Indeed, a Danish investigator lived for a whole year on a diet comprised solely of potatoes and kept fit and well.

Susie Gentille can tell you all this in fewer words. You can't miss her, seated on her wooden stool, just as you enter the outdoor food arcade from the parking lot. In summertime, her feet dangle in soft cloth slippers, stockings knotted below the knees. In wintertime she rocks forward on the stool, wrapping her legs around the coal brazier that glows beneath her perch. The "Potato Lady," at 82, is the oldest vendor in the Market; she never misses a day presiding over her potato boutique.

"The Doctor told me to stay home because I have heart trouble. I said, 'Listen, I'm going to the Market. If I gotta die, I'll die with company.'"

SUSIE GENTILLE

I can take it. Those others can't take it. Because I come from the Old Country people. I am Slovak, even though I've been married all my life to an Italian. My mother used to work in buildings, scrubbing on her hands and knees. She used to leave the house about four in the afternoon and come back about two in the morning. Now they've got everything with electricity. How would you like it on your hands and knees? I'm 82 years old and I have been working every minute of my life. I was born in 1899. When I was 16, I got married and came to work with my husband in the Market. Even before that, I used to come to the Market on Saturdays to visit him here. Then I got the children and I had to stay home.

My husband always wanted to be the first one down here at the Market, so he'd bring the boys, asleep in the wagon, waiting for the Market lights to go on. Before we had the truck, we had a wagon with horses. There was a barn out behind the house. My husband had to clean the horses and I had to clean the stables and I stunk from manure. I had to go on a streetcar to come to help in the stand and you can imagine how I smelled. You know how manure smells. I used to be embarrassed, but I couldn't help it. As soon as the children were big enough, I came back to the Market full time and I've been here ever since.

Oh, except once we went on a vacation, my husband and I. A friend of ours took us to Canada. My father-in-law told us to go and have a good time for once. We went to St. Anne's Shrine. While we were gone, my brother-in-law passed away. And we never saw him again; they buried him before we came back. And, after that, my husband, he had a heart attack and he kept suffering with his heart and then he died of a

142

heart attack. That killed him. We should have **never** gone. That was my one vacation.

Now I'm the oldest one in the Market. I enjoy the people; I feel good when I'm here. They call me "Grandma," or "Grandmother," and I like that. The doctor told me to stay home because I have heart trouble. He said, "You don't go to the Market." I said, "Listen, I'm going to the Market; you're not going to tell me to stay home." If I gotta die, I'll die with company. Here in the Market, I'm not going to die by myself.

The customers always greet me. When I was in the hospital to have the operation on my eyes, they all missed me. I got cards. A lot of people said, "Oh, I'm so glad you're back. How do you feel? Hi, Mom." And that makes you feel good, you know. That's why I like to be out here.

But the vendors — they are not the same as before. We used to be like one family, looking out for each other. We all sold for the same price. If he had it for so much, we had it for so much. Not any less, not any more. But, now it's different. These vendors that look so nice in front of you — they're nice and then they double-cross. They come around here and they look at the prices and they change their prices. Even for a penny. Like look over there. He's got ten pounds for ninety-nine cents and we got ten pounds for a dollar.

We have four kinds of potatoes. We've got the all-purpose, we've got the russets, we've got the reds and we've got the Idahos. The all-purpose, the russets and the reds you can do anything with them: you can bake them, fry them, mash them. But, the Idahos, if the lady is busy with the housework and she boils them too long, sometimes they fall apart.

For 66 years, summer, winter I'm always out here. I'm never cold because I dress real warm. And we have the little charcoal burner if my feet get bad. I feel best outside. The only time I went inside was once when someone heard on the radio that the end of the world was coming, something like that. So, they all made me go inside the Markethouse by Victor who has the grocery stand. My son insisted. The radio announced that everyone should go under cover. Maybe it was a tornado or something. I was inside there for about an hour, but nothing happened. So, I came back outside. I have never been inside again.

Wednesdays I get up at five; Fridays and Saturdays I get up at four. I set my alarm clock but I don't need it because I'm always up before it rings. I get up, I put my coffee on, I wash myself and then I go in the front room and say my prayers. When I get through with my prayers, then I call up my son, William, and Johnny the helper and I finish my prayers in the kitchen.

I have to say my prayers before I go to the Market, because when I come home, I'm too tired. I say my rosary every morning for about an hour, sometimes and hour and a half. You see, I've got different Novena books. On Mondays I pray to Our Lady of the Miraculous Medal at St. Anne's; Tuesdays I pray to St. Anthony and St. Frances; Wednesdays I pray to St. Joseph; Thursdays I pray to St. Jude; Fridays I pray to St. Frances Xavier Cabrini; Saturdays I pray to St. Theresa, Little Flower of Jesus; Sundays I pray to the Blessed Mother. My Novenas I say in the front room. In the kitchen I have different prayers I say to the same saints.

I ask God to help and bless me and my family. Well, so far it works — I'm here. I'm the oldest one in all my family — from my mother's side, from my father's side, from my in-laws' side. I'm the only one that's the longest.

PORTRAIT OF THREE GENERATIONS

Three generations of the Gentille family stand together, maintaining the long tradition of their outdoor Market stand. Susie Gentille and her son William and her grandson Charles sell potatoes and onions — come hail or high water.

"Being your own boss — that's ninety percent of it."

WILLIAM GENTILLE AND HIS SON, CHARLES

WILLIAM: My father's father, he started it. Four generations of us working in this Market. My grandfather, my father and mother, myself and now my son Charles. Our first specialty was bananas. We also sold oranges, lemons, grapefruit. This Market was home to everybody. They were all old timers, they were all from the same neighborhoods — people that came in on the same boat together. Half of them couldn't even speak the right English. They were all Italians; 99.9 percent were Italian. That's all they knew: fruits and vegetables.

When I was a kid, I remember coming down here at midnight in the truck with my father and my older brother. Sitting in that truck across the

Susie Gentille's grandson flaunts the family name.

street, waiting for the Market to open so we could set up. "The first one, the early bird, catches the worm," my father used to say. It was terrible when it was five below zero and there was no heat. But my father didn't believe in heat so we never had any heaters.

We hung the huge bunches of bananas on a special hook and there was a curved knife to cut them down. But about 20 years ago our banana man made it tough for us to buy. All of a sudden if we wanted the bananas, we had to give him a dollar a bunch extra, plus we were forced to buy oranges or lemons or whatever he was stuck with on that day. That got to be too expensive.

That's when we switched to potatoes and onions. That's been our specialty ever since. We carry Number One potatoes; we carry Commercial. The Number Ones are hand graded; they don't have all the little cuts and bruises on them. We carry the Commercials for big families that can't afford otherwise. Potatoes have a different character depending on where they are grown. Ohio and Pennsylvania potatoes tend to be a little more watery — they don't irrigate. Now, Idaho is the only state that irrigates. That's why Idahos are always fluffier, always better.

CHARLES: Before I came down here to work with my father, I worked once in a big potato processing plant. They used to get them in loose in boxcars — 190,000 pounds of potatoes in a car. They'd shovel them in and wash them and then we'd box them up, dry them, peel them.

WILLIAM: Speaking about a load of potatoes, a man came to our stand last fall — you could tell he was from the Old Country — he bought over 500 pounds of potatoes and buried them in a hole in his backyard, some kind of root cellar where he was going to keep them all winter, just like in the old days. When I worked for Ohio Provision for a while, I worked with a fellow who came from the Old Country. He'd eat a slice of bread and a dish of potatoes and that was his

146

supper. The Lord lived on water for 40 days; you can sure live on potatoes.

I know this fellow who became a rich man because of potatoes. Potatoes didn't lead to his success; the **eating** of the potatoes led to his success. He came over here during the Hungarian Revolution and he had nothing but the skin on his back. When he first came to the Market, he couldn't even afford a potato. So, I gave him a potato. Then he went to work. This guy used to come every week and buy 150 to 200 pounds of potatoes. Potatoes for breakfast, lunch and dinner; a pound of Kielbasa for seven people and 25 pounds of potatoes. So, the first few years he was here that's how he saved every penny he earned; he really pulled himself up. I would say within three years he had two two-family houses and he was building himself a new single home in Parma. Now the guy is a millionaire.

And me, I'm selling him the potatoes, and I still have to get up at four in the morning to earn a living! But, I don't mind because I have nobody to tell me what to do in this work. Being your own boss, that's 90 percent of it. So, I'll stick with the Market. Now, my son Charles here — he sees himself on Lauderdale Beach.

CHARLES: I won't be here in this Market in ten years. Me, I can't take this life. Listen, I've got a bad back and if I sneeze wrong, I wind up in the hospital. Well, I might make it here for another ten years.

"It used to be you could look
into a bakery window
and almost tell by the
decorating on the cake
who was working in the bakery."

ALBERT JENSCH

A baker all his life, Albert Jensch kneads his hands together while shaping his early recollections into words. His father, Max Jensch, had one of the original bakery stands in the West Side Market, Parma Home Bakery. Today, the stand is owned by others and operates under the name, Angie's. Over the years each son in the family took his turn standing vigil, keeping the fires going in the family ovens.

Retired from the bakery business for health reasons, Albert the youngest baker son, still delights in the recitation of recipes prepared as holiday treats. The artistic skills he acquired enhanced his life; the strict routines he followed controlled his life. The smallest detail in the daily bakery ritual filters through the haze of flour dust and still appears to him as vivid as the raisin on the face of the gingerbread man.

IT'S funny, sometimes you'll do something when you're a child that sticks with you. I must have been five years old, playing around in our bakery. There was a big kettle of marshmallow that was used as filling in cream rolls and pastries, and there was a rack of breads next to it. Whatever made me do it, I don't know, but I reached in the kettle and smeared marshmallow all over the breads. I can still hear my father hollering, "Who did that?" Well, all they had to do was take a look at me and it was a dead giveaway.

My father was always very fussy; everything had to be right. Maybe sometimes we would cross our legs or put a leg up — he'd kick us in the leg and say, "You got two good feet. Stand on them." Or, if you got one hand in your pockets, "What's the matter? Your hands cold? Get your hands out of your pockets!" It's not like kids nowadays who have a choice of things. No, we had to do it — period! Because you just didn't talk back to people those days. When we were kids, we would go somewhere and we would sit down on a chair. And you sat on that chair and you kept your mouth shut until someone talked to you. Then you could answer.

The trouble was, my father was an old German. And he put into us what was put into him: work. When you'd complain, he'd say, "Be satisfied you've got a roof over your head, you've got something to eat." In the Old Country I guess there were times when they didn't have that. My parents were both very, very hard workers. We always lived right over the bakery and my mother worked in the bakery, she worked in the store, she worked in the house. She had bad legs, varicose veins thicker than my finger. Long hours, standing on her feet. I think of that sometimes. Boy, what price glory!

Ours was a family business. I knew no other way of life. I can't say whether I enjoyed it or didn't enjoy it — see, I was brought up under it. How would a kid know anything different unless he went off to college and got other ideas. We weren't even allowed to finish high school because it was Depression days. I don't think I ever really resented not being able to finish high school except the few times when kids I knew who had all graduated together had class reunions. I kind of felt left out — I completed the tenth and that was that.

By the time I was 16 years old I was a pretty good baker. When we were making doughnuts, if one doughnut in the dough form was a little thicker or a little thinner than it should be, my father would throw it back and say, "Make it right." You became more meticulous in your work.

My father had a philosophy that you learn from other people. We would hire bakers and learn skills from them. One man we had working for us was very good at cake decorating. I asked him to teach me. He'd show me how to make one type of border, using a pastry bag, then he'd correct me and tell me to practice it. A day or two later, I'd show him what I'd practiced and if he said, "Okay, you've got it good," then he'd show me another detail. So gradually I learned.

It used to be you could look into a bakery window and almost tell by the decorating on the cake who was working in the bakery. You see, the bakery business was based on apprenticeship. But, that tradition ran into a little problem having to do with the rising cost of labor, brought about by the unions. The old-timers were getting older, going on their way, so we'd have to bring in younger blood to learn from them. If a kid was coming in after school to do cleaning work and he showed an interest in the bakery art, we'd encourage him. Of course, the union would say if the kid's going to do this, he's got to join the union. But we got to know the guys pretty well, and convinced them to wait until the kid was out of school. If he was still interested, **then** they got him. In the meanwhile, we were teaching him a trade. We got along that way.

Well, at that time, a kid started out at 75 dollars a week and every six months he would get an increase in pay according to the union scale. At the end of two years, they classified him as a full-fledged journeyman, getting a full-fledged pay. You've got a man working for you who has been a baker all his life. He's a first class man so you give him 125 dollars. Now this youngster comes along who is only in it two years and the union says he gets 125 dollars. So, can you see the hard feelings immediately? This old-timer says, "You mean that kid still wet behind the ears is getting just like I'm getting?" It was a terrible blow to his pride.

In our bakery operation everything was scheduling. The cycle started up at night and about noontime the next day they'd finish up. They used to fire the ovens with wood and coke, then later switched to gas. The object was to heat up the bricks which lined the inside of the oven. The firebox was down below it. But it was hard to control the heat — your oven was either too hot or too cold. They always baked the bread first because that needed a hotter oven: 400 to 500 degrees. For cakes and cookies your oven had to be a little bit cooler so that was the last thing to be baked. A man would come in about eight in the evening and mix doughs. At that time, they mixed the dough by hand in a wooden trough. He would add the flour, the other ingredients, stir it up a little and then add the water to it. Then he had to stoop over and mix it by hand. That's why many an old-timer used to have "flour asthma" because his face was always in that trough — he'd be breathing that flour.

Then you'd allow maybe two, three hours for that dough, by the time it was mixed and fermented, to rise up. When the yeast starts working the dough maybe triples in size, then it would be ready to be worked into individual breads. By that time a couple more men would come in to work on that dough that had been preparing and they would "throw the dough on a bench." If they were going to make bread, each loaf had to be weighed, so they'd take a scraper and chop the dough off into little pieces and then they would round those pieces up and leave them to relax maybe ten minutes. Then they would form them into loaves of bread. All hand work. Everybody — Spang, Laub Bakeries, they were all starting out at that time — we all had to go through the same procedure.

The men were all spaced on different shifts and they would put the bread in the brick ovens. They would place the loaves on a "peel" which is a wooden paddle with a long handle. They'd put a little cornmeal on that peel so the dough would slide off; they would pick up maybe three or four loaves at a time and shove that peel way in the oven, then they'd give it just the right jerk. That was a trick, to jerk it off right, because you had to get 200 loaves of bread in that oven and you had to learn to place those in correctly or you would only get maybe 100 or 150 loaves in there, which is not good.

Most all bread was baked on the hearth, on the actual stones. And that gives a different taste to bread. Except white bread was baked in a pan. We made a pumpernickel bread that was also baked in a special wood-lined pan because the dough couldn't touch metal. My father was the only one who could put that pan form together, who had the patience. The slats of wood that had to line the pan were not uniform and one of his jobs when he was getting older was to line up those pieces of wood in the pan, grease them with a little lard so we could make the individual loaves. Later on with the union and higher labor costs we couldn't afford to pay a man just to horse around with those wood slats so we looked for shortcuts to make the pumpernickel a different way.

The Market was a lifeline always — we always had a stand down there to sell our line of baked goods. My father got rid of the horse and wagon and got an old Model T Ford truck to deliver our baked goods. An old German aunt ran the stand in the Market for us. We had to get up real early in the morning on Saturdays to pack all the boxes and trays on the truck; we had to get down to that Markethouse by six at least, otherwise we wouldn't get a parking place along the loading dock. Oh, there was a battle with those produce guys! A lot of times you'd be maneuvering to back in to the dock and one of those outside guys would zoom into your parking space. There were more fights that way.

Saturday night we always got down there a little earlier to start packing up. There were always people walking around looking for bargains because at the end of the day if we had a surplus maybe we would cut the prices in half rather than take the stuff home and they knew it. People would just walk up, "Anything cheap yet?" "No, not yet." After a while, we'd have to reduce the price.

Betty Bade, the Candy Lady, had the stand right next to us in the Markethouse. Her father had invented a gadget: a fly chaser. He had rigged a rod going across the top of his stand and every three feet along the overhead rod he attached a rod coming down. Fixed to these hanging rods were thin strips of paper, like confetti. He had the whole apparatus hooked up to a motor and when he turned it on the rods would swing back and forth swishing the confetti to keep the flies away. We contributed our part to it and extended the contraption across the front of our two stands; we were the only ones in the Markethouse who had the fly machine. When Betty Bade relocated on the center aisle we took over her space and the fly chaser remained with us. Flies used to be a problem down there in the summertime; that was quite an invention.

When we sold the stand to Angie Tabaco she renamed it "Angie's" and to this day it carries her name even though she's retired. Angie had worked for us — she managed the stand and she used to help out in our store so she was familiar with the whole operation. She continued to get her baked goods from us as long as we kept the bakery.

We used to keep a book with all the special recipes for the holidays. Take Christmas. We made a special German bread called "hutzel brot." In a rye dough we put cherries, raisins, nuts, prunes, dried apricots, dried pears. We'd get all that fruit from Roberto's by the case and it was really a job pitting and cutting the fruit up in little pieces. We always had fun displaying that beautiful bread; we cut some loaves in half and showed them on the counter.

For Easter we used to make an Easter lamb. When we had 100 or 200 lamb shaped cakes baked then we'd have to proceed to decorate them. We'd put them out on a cardboard, beat up a special butter cream and cover the whole lamb, shape it up. It was a pain in the neck, because those darn ears would come off, or the head would break. Then you'd put coconut around it to look like fur. Then you would have to take a little bag of butter cream, and put a mouth on it, put two eyes on it and then you'd tie a ribbon around it, put each lamb in a plastic bag to keep it fresh and put them in a cake box. All that took a tremendous amount of patience.

I still love decorating cookies for the family. My wife and I get started a couple weeks before Christmas to get it all done. I eat very little bread now. Once in a while I enjoy a loaf of rye bread. When I eat bread, I like to eat it plain. No butter or anything.

ALLEN C. HOLMES

Epicurus, the ancient Greek philosopher, was a Citizen of Athens who inspired many to embrace the Truth and Beauty he defined.

Allen C. Holmes is a Citizen of Cleveland and inspires many to embrace the causes of Truth and Beauty HE supports. A distinguished lawyer, he serves his profession with brilliance; a patron of the arts, he serves his community's cultural institutions with devotion. The performing, visual and academic arts are graced by his presence; he serves as a member of the boards of trustees of the Cleveland Institute of Art, the Cleveland Institute of Music, WVIZ-TV and Case Western Reserve University.

But he particularly delights in his affiliations that reflect his gourmet interests for, like a true Epicurean, he is a connoisseur of the many delights of the senses. He derives pleasure from the eating of fine foods and the drinking of fine wines. He takes pride in being a member of the North American Committee of the International Wine and Food Society, the Cleveland Chapter of Chevaliers du Tastevin and Les Amies du Vin.

Traveling the world in pursuit of a special vintage wine or a special rare dining adventure, he returns faithfully to Cleveland's West Side Market where for 25 years he has enjoyed the shopping. He bounds from vendor to vendor, plucking up exotic ingredients for a complicated recipe he has in hand. This ebullient and elegant personage responds with as much glee to a perfectly ripened fig as he does to a perfectly played fugue.

LOUISE and I have our favorite ritual when we arrive at the Markethouse: we always buy a little sandwich for our breakfast — a nice bratwurst with sauerkraut on a fresh roll. Then I get a glass of buttermilk from the dairy stand; it's kept nice and cold. See, they keep the salt over there if you want it. — How are you today? I need some buttermilk! — We're always down here around seven on Saturday mornings because I must go on to my office from here. If we arrive as late as eight o'clock at the Market, that means we slept in!

We're going to be at home tonight, which is a delightful treat for us. We've got our dinner all planned. We'll start with soup because I **love** soups. When our children were at home, they liked to make a stockpot and then create various soups using it. I like to invent dishes, such as braised endive with celeriac or dishes with salsify. We love to consult about a menu and often come over here with our recipe book in hand.

I love avocados. I was debating about having these avocados with a dressing on them. No — we're going to make a guacamole. Of course, we like our guacamole spicy; it's excellent spread on bread along with that salted fish roe. We're going to have to use these avocados right away; they'll have to be used up tonight or they'll go bad.

We try to stay with the seasonal things — like these beautiful eggplants here. They don't have any soft spots and are firm; they'll come around very promptly. What I like to do is sauté them on our grill. We put some oil on them and dust them with a little flour; that way they don't get too soaked.

Of course, we're going to have cheeses. We have to be careful to get the right kinds to complement the wine we'll be drinking. Chèvre

Now for our menu this evening — of course we'll have some of the lovely sausages we just bought. Bismarck remarked upon an occasion, "You should never let your mother or your children see **sausages** or **laws** being made!" I think that is very good advice. The white veal sausage isn't as nice this time of year. It's a seasonal thing and usually in the spring when the animals are young they're tastier. The sausages that are good are beautifully white. This stand has the most beautiful veal; if you want to have a veal stew, this is the place. Breast of veal — the best in town.

This morning as we came through the aisles, someone said hello. I told Louise that was one of the volunteer workers who helped in the United Way. When I was the general chairman of the United Way campaign a few years ago, several of the volunteers whom I met said, "Well, since you go to the Market, I'll work with you!" They must have felt I was okay because they saw me here. And they're right — we recognize each other here. We all come at the same time every week and we look out for each other.

There's a great esprit here, the bantering back and forth. This place keeps a lot of ties alive. People move out into other neighborhoods, then they come back here to see each other. My goodness, people flock in here from Strongsville, Brooklyn, and Parma and North Ridgeville. We've been coming to Market for 25 years; it's a very exciting place to be. Just to see all those magnificent vegetables stacked here, the beautiful colors. When we have guests from out of the City, we bring them to the Market and they're delighted and impressed.

You can find things here that are simply not available any place else. You see the sweetbreads over there; this is one of the few places in town where you can always buy them. That stand has nice rabbit. We love rabbit; we come looking for it in the fall. It goes in a beautiful cream sauce or you can use a hunter's sauce, you know — forestière — but it really tastes best

and certain other goat cheeses that I love would overwhelm a delicate wine. That's what's so great about shopping here at the Market. I stop to see one of the cheese men, we chat and I get some cheeses he recommends. Then I go across to see another favorite cheese expert. You know, there are several kinds of feta — Bulgarian, the Greek — she will advise me as to which is the best. She'll say this is better for salads and don't use this. The vendors are very good about giving advice.

in a dill sauce. Some of the trends in gourmet eating that have caught on widely were started in the Market. We love oxtail ragout very much and this is the place for oxtail. We often think in terms of what wines go — for example, the oxtail goes so beautifully with some of those big Rhône wines, which are absolutely splendid. We're drinking the 1970 Rhônes right now and they're **just** magnificent!

The Markethouse butchers have all kinds of delicacies you just can't find anywhere else. I love the whole lamb's head; you eat the whole thing. When I was out in San Francisco recently, I had it served in a vinaigrette. It has so many different tastes in it. Brains vinaigrette is also a great delicacy — I just love brains.

Now, we'll have to have some figs for dessert after the cheeses — I'm eyeing some over here. Louise likes them not too ripe and I like them **very** ripe — yes, we'll have two of each, please — and they go so beautifully with a nice Sauternes; I'll use a 1971 Château Suduiraut for the dessert wine tonight.

Oh, the candied ginger here is the best. We use a lot of that in various dishes; it's a fascinating ingredient. A great combination is candied ginger and cheese; it sets off a cheese magnificently. You have no idea what a thing it is. Also, candied ginger ice cream is the best; we used to make it when the boys were home. I love to get those enormous macaroon cookies at the pastry stand and break them up over a dish of ginger ice cream or a Bavarian cream. They give quite a different texture.

We have a fairly heavy breakfast on Sunday because we come here so regularly and get tempted. We're going to have creamed chipped beef tomorrow morning and some of that slab bacon. It is almost impossible to find real chipped beef anymore but at this stand their chipped beef is genuine. — Good morning, your chipped beef. Well, today I think maybe about half a pound is good. — I have to be honest about it, we cheat a little bit and have a nice dry Muscadet for breakfast sometimes; we always have a nice dry wine that sets off some of these rich items. Some Saturdays we come over here and buy codfish and then have creamed codfish for breakfast or we'll have the sausages and corned beef hash. Our children often come in on us; we have four sons and they descend on us from Washington, Houston, New York.

Next week we're having guests in for dinner and I'm going to serve three different champagnes to begin. One, the Cuvée William from the Deutz Vineyards, I rate with the top three in the world. I'll put the champagne glasses out on the sideboard and see if my guests know what they're drinking. Then they've got to taste all the reds and tell me what they're like. I'll be offering one red that is very, very rare, a 1959 Monopôle, La Tache. There are very few bottles of that left anywhere in the world.

Basically, you learn about wine by drinking it. We've consumed a lot of wine and that's the way we learn. Next month we'll be in France — the 26th of September is the night of the equinox and we'll be dining near Beaune at the Château Clos de Vougeot. The equinoctial banquet of the Chaevaliers du Tastevin is one of the great events they have every year. The equinox is the critical date in the wine country; what happens in the vineyards in September determines what kind of year they will have. This year has had a bad beginning; there were some heavy losses in certain parts of Burgundy because of hail storms that came through. We're all very concerned.

You know, last night after attending the orchestra concert at Blossom, Louise and I were talking about the two types of art: perishable and enduring. We seem to crave especially those things that are perishable, like a great concert or a great meal. One could draw parallels between a symphony and a dinner even down to the form each takes — the four movements. Perishability provides piquancy to life; something that lasts forever is not as thrilling to us. A great meal is just like that concert performance last night.

"I can remember that all the old-time cash registers had a separate compartment with a lock and key to keep the gold pieces."

FREDERICK J. WEIGEL

Weigel's Meats was always known as specialists in beef, pork and veal. Although Frederick Weigel is retired now, his lifetime of interest in the Market has marked him as quite a history buff. Through intensive studying and searching he has collected a treasure-trove of West Side Market memorabilia; newspaper clippings and trade journals are stashed in boxes in his study, photographs and personal documents are piled all over his desk.

Fred's vivid remembering tracks back more than 130 years to tell of four generations of Weigels evolving through the meat business. His great-grandfather, the cattle drover; his grandfather, the slaughterer; his father, the butcher; himself, the merchant.

IT was 1848 and my great-grandfather had to get out of Germany in a hurry; he was worried he'd get hanged as an anarchist. He was mixed up with Carl Schurz in the uprising that led to the German Revolution of 1848-49. **Great-grandfather Fred and Schurz fled to America** where Carl Schurz became a famous American: a strong anti-slavery advocate, a senator, a dedicated reformer. But Fred Weigel didn't dabble much in politics; he was a drover. In those days, that's what they called the men who drove the cattle. He settled in Parma in the 1850s to earn his living and to raise his family.

His son, my Grandfather Fred, grew up to take a different interest in the cattle business; about 1882 he bought six or eight acres on the corner of what is now West 32nd Street and Meyer Avenue and set up a slaughterhouse. Grandfather Fred had a flash of style about him; he always wore a bowler hat and carried a whip. Until the turn of the century there was quite a community of slaughterhouses in that area because of the ideal lay of the land. A little creek ran right down through the field there. When they slaughtered the cattle, the pigs and the sheep, the blood would run into that little creek and then into a bigger creek and eventually flowed red into the Cuyahoga River. After a while, the City of Cleveland decided that was a very unsanitary way of doing business.

Each slaughterhouse ran a small retail meat market along with its operation to serve the local neighborhood. The Bohemians who lived in that neighborhood and worked in the woolen mills down the street wanted their meat fresh for the Sunday meal. So, Sunday morning became the busiest time of the week. Grandfather Fred would open up at five A.M. and by one he would be sold out.

Fred Weigel displays the antique marker from his family's stand.

There was no refrigeration in those days so the stuff had to be sold immediately. My dad told me that when he was a young boy around 1890, he had the job of loading the slaughtered carcasses on a little butcher wagon and taking them over to the old Central Market where the butchers ran a wholesale market on the curb outside. They would bring the sides of beef over and hang them on racks and sell right in the street.

After the City closed down those slaughterhouses because of the water pollution, the industry moved over to West 65th Street area which became known as the Cleveland Stockyards. The old railroad track is still there. The cattle would be shipped in and herded directly off the boxcars into pens. The packers would bid on them at auction and they would be killed right there on the street. The smell is something you don't forget.

My grandfather decided to just stick with running his small meat market in the old neighborhood and my father came to work with him. My Uncle Johnny Koenigshoff was a more ambitious member of the family and he developed a tremendous meat business in the Old Central Market. He was a glamour boy and a great salesman. He was the patron saint of the Pepper Saloon and reached the height of his

Weigel's meat stand, ready for business in 1912.

fame when they painted his portrait in oil and hung it behind the bar. From my understanding, it is still there.

When Uncle Johnny came in, nobody bought a drink — he bought all the drinks. So, consequently, he had a lot of friends and he did the biggest business in the market. He had an "in" with the old Cleveland Provision Company, located on the banks of the Cuyahoga River. Johnny would come in wearing his swell raglan coat with big pockets filled with five-dollar bills. Every time he would see somebody who could do him some good, he'd hand out a five-dollar bill. So, consequently, Johnny Koenigshoff got the finest Wilshire hams and the finest pork loins and did the biggest business.

When the new West Side Markethouse opened in 1912, Uncle Johnny was the first one in there. Even though the new Markethouse was then considered (and probably still is) the most modern and beautiful municipal food market in the world, people were awed with it and at first seemed to shy away from the magnificent new structure. After about six months, Uncle John felt there wasn't enough action for him. So my dad took over the stand and is counted among the original tenants. He lived to be the oldest of that special group.

Weigels: specialists in pork, beef and veal. My dad would pile the pork loins and picnic hams up high on the marble counters to make it look attractive. Some sharpshooters were sure to come along and want the one on the bottom. They'd pull that out and the whole damn pile would fall down on the floor. We would have to wipe it off and pile it back up again.

The counters were beautiful Carrara marble imported from Italy. But, they were vulnerable. In those days, the cutting was done right on the counter because the coolers were not set up for such work. Once in a while somebody would be careless and drop a side of beef on the marble slab and it would crack. That was an expensive proposition. One of the reasons the West Side

Market House Association was formed by the tenants in 1915 was so they could set up their own insurance fund to cover such costly replacements. My father was one of the charter members of that group and our family was always proud to take an active role in the Association's activities over all the years.

We had one particular merchant who was quite a big show-off and was one of the richest men in the Market. This old tyrant had a poor relative working for him, a little guy called "Cooney." To show off, he would say, "Cooney, this lady wants to see what a hindquarter of beef looks like. Run downstairs and get one." So, Cooney would run down the stairs to the cooler and come struggling up with a hindquarter that weighed about 150 pounds. "There's a hindquarter of beef, Missus. Now you know. Okay, Cooney, now take it back down." He liked to show off his authority.

The stand next to this tyrant was run by a nice widow lady. Nobody ever thought he had any romance in his soul, but she accused him of breach of promise because he used to "cooler kiss" her up and down the stairway! I think she settled for a couple of thousand dollars. That was known as the Cooler Kissing Romance.

I started in helping my dad in the Market about 1922, when I was about 11 or 12 years old. I can remember that all the oldtime cash registers had the wide slot to hold the big old bills and every register had a separate compartment with a lock and key to keep the gold pieces. Gold pieces used to circulate up until 1932, which reminds me of one old customer we had. Her name was Hoag; she ran a boarding house over on Franklin Avenue. She carried her money, usually gold pieces, in a leather pouch, well hidden down in her bosom. She'd lean over, reach way in and pull out her gold. After she had made her purchase and paid, her husband would invariably come back and ask us to loan him two dollars. We knew he wanted to go to the beer joint, so we always let him take a couple of bucks. She always paid us back.

Later, during World War II, when meat got so scarce, the cuts to find were those that didn't require any ration points. I had a little beat-up truck and I'd get up at two in the morning and I'd go down to the packing houses to look for things that were no points like livers and hearts and neckbones, backbones. I had an old meat grinder with a bell and I'd holler "No points!" It would go just as fast as you could put it out. People would line up early in the morning to buy neckbones. There wasn't any meat on them at all.

It was fun doing business. It was **fun** merchandising; I felt like a big wheel at times. We all had pranks we played on unsuspecting customers. I recall how we sometimes passed off a wad of cheesecloth for a piece of tripe when a drunk wandered in late on a Saturday. And, then there was the black beef. When an animal was overheated before it was slaughtered, the meat would turn a dark color and didn't look very appetizing even though it was extremely tender. It was hard to sell these discolored hindquarters. So, sometimes we would display a nice red steak in front and conceal the "black" beef behind the scale. When the customer pointed to what she wanted, we would switch it for a dark piece while we were wrapping it up. One day, an irate customer showed up and intoned: "No switch-ee on me, you son of a bitch-ee. . . I want **that** one!"

I enjoyed doing business and to tell the truth, I enjoyed making money. I can honestly say the Markethouse was good to us and we were good to the Market. Everyone loved my dad. Old Eddie Weigel had so many friends he couldn't stay away. When he died in 1971 at the age of 93, he had just come home from visiting the Market.

Grandfather Weigel's slaughterhouse, in 1870, was located on the corner of Meyer Avenue and Louis Street (now called West 32nd Street).

Grandfather Weigel
at home, around
the corner from
the slaughterhouse.

"I think it's really
a personality game.
Either the customer is attracted to
you, or you are attracted to him.
That's what it is."

IRENE DEVER

Irene Dever and her daughter, Diane, smiling out at the crowd, could be re-enacting a classic Lux Soap Commercial. Although they are both blonde and beautiful, they are more likely to attribute their fine complexions to hard physical work rather than soft soap. Irene stars in the role of "child of the Market," having started working here at the age of nine. Now her child, Diane, joins the ranks of a new generation of Market kids who have chosen to make their career the carrying on of the family tradition.

OUR family lived on Abbey, right on the corner, and when I was nine years old, I came up here to the Market and started shelling lima beans and peas to make extra spending money. There used to be a lot of us kids out there; you could go up to a stand outside anytime and ask for something to do and they would put you to work. I got two or three cents a quart, shelling beans and peas.

As I grew up, I always kept at least a small job here at the Market, even when I worked at the telephone company, and after I got married I'd come down here on Saturdays to work for the lunch meat stand.

About nine years ago, when I had the chance to buy this stand, I didn't know if I could handle it. I was going to be 40, and I figured that I was kind of old to start out in business. But I took it anyhow; I haven't regretted a day of it.

This was basically a butter, cheese, and eggs stand and we added more stuff to it. We feature unusual salads and marinated vegetables. Marinated artichoke hearts, mushrooms and peppers, stuffed baby eggplants, health salads. Then, of course, we have the exclusive on the home-made pirogies from Sts. Peter and Paul Ukrainian Catholic Church. The church ladies make mountains of pirogies every week to raise money for the church and they buy the dry cheese from us. We give them a break on the price of the cheese and they give me the exclusive on their pirogies to sell in our stand.

We have a busy stand and I guess that's half the battle. I think it's really a personality game. Either the customer is attracted to you or you are attracted to him. That's what it is. We really try to cater to people; I think sometimes we overdo it a little bit, then they get mad when we're not here. They come and tell me all their problems and think I can help out. We have a cheese that has no salt in it and when a customer on a special diet tries it he thinks, Good, I can have that. But I always ask them to check with their doctor first because I am not a medical person.

Diane and I run the stand ourselves. My daughter has been helping since she was 12. When she got out of school about three years ago, she came to work with me full time. Now she wants to make a career of this. Diane is the runner — she does all the running up and down to the cooler, picking up supplies and orders. She's a very good helper; she's my **number one** man.

A labor of love is performed by the ladies of Sts. Peter and Paul Ukrainian Catholic Church in their effort to raise needed monies for the Church. In this weekly ritual, they prepare, cook and offer for sale **pirogies.** These voluptuous delicacies are filled with a choice of cottage cheese, mashed potato, prune lekvar or sauerkraut.

The separate tasks are accomplished in an informal assembly-line: the dough is kneaded in an old porcelain bathtub, then rolled out through an old-fashioned washing machine wringer. A glass jelly jar turned upside-down is the imple-ment used to stamp out the dough. The perfect circles of dough are then deftly tossed across the room to the next echelon of women seated behind long tables. Spooning from mountains of cheese, potato, prune or sauerkraut, they carefully fill and pinch shut each custom-made pirogi. This toil continues all through the night so that the pirogies can be boiled in huge pots, ready the next day for the devoted customers who line up with pots and plastic containers they have brought to carry home the precious treats.

"...The superintendent of the
Market took me into the saloon
where no colored were seen,
and he told all the guys,
'This man works for me, you treat
him just like everyone else.'"

JESSE BRADLEY

The monumental figure hunched on the loading dock looking like a badly-eroded sandstone sculpture is Jesse Bradley. He is the foreman of the Market, responsible for the comings and goings of the place. If the elevator sticks, if the roof leaks, if a truck blocks the ramp — Jesse knows. But within the hulking ruin of this once-great athlete resides a gentle observer who knows something else: the small painful stories of the bums and bag ladies who hover around the edges of his bustling dock.

The market place has always been home to the seer, foretelling the inevitable and sometimes the remarkable. Jesse, like Tiresias, the blind soothsayer of ancient Greece, sits slightly offstage in his tiny office, knowing all. He sees with remarkable clarity the profound human condition of the drunks, the derelicts who inhabit the shadow of the great Markethouse. Jesse's words fall from between the soft cushions of his toothless gums, muffling the harsh message — like the muddled riddle of the oracle.

MY father came up from Alabama — Montgomery — in 1922. During the First World War he was the boss of the wrecking crew for the New York Central Railroad but after the war a new superintendent took the job away from him. He got mad. His brothers were in Cleveland and they told him this was a nice place, his kids could get good schooling. He decided to come.

My father got a job with the New York Central Railroad here, but every time my mother was ready to have a baby she went back to her people in Alabama where she felt more at home. We lived in a mostly Jewish neighborhood and there were no problems. I was the only colored boy in my room in Woolrich School at 62nd and Kinsman; there was no racial tension whatsoever.

When we needed a bigger house to live in my father sent my grandfather out to rent the upstairs of a nice two-family. (My grandfather was a white fella.) When we all showed up to move into the house, the man said, "You can't live here; I rented this place to an old white man." My father told him, "That's my **father!**" We lived in that house for 25 years.

I was a big boy and when I went out for football in high school the coach put me as a blocking guard. They had big hopes for me and raised money to buy me a special helmet, but I got more hurt with that thing on than without it! During my time, there weren't any colored playing in the Big Ten colleges. Ozzie Simmons was the only one; he played for Iowa. I won a scholarship to Vanderbilt University. On the application my picture showed me up to be white. They sent a scout up to see me and when he came he said, "We made a mistake." I knew it was a mistake in the **beginning** — I mean, Vanderbilt

was in Tennessee! At that time, what were you gonna do, fight it? It was fate, that's all. I could have gotten a scholarship to all the colored colleges but I wouldn't go because they didn't rate in big-time football.

During the second World War I found myself working for Thompson Products. We had lived around that plant area for 25 years; I had an uncle had his finger sliced off there back in 1926. When you live in a neighborhood all your life, everybody looks out for you. The man at the draft board told me, "Bradley, if you get into a war plant, we won't bother you." I was working for the New York Central with my father, but the draft board rated that only 60 percent essential and to stay out of the draft I had to be in 90 percent. My father nearly bust a gut because he worked for the railroad for 62 years since he was 12 years old, and he thought the railroad was the **only** job. He said, "The railroad works when nothing else works." But he lived long enough to see everything go down.

So, I went to work at Thompson Products in expediting. I had been there about a month when Fred Crawford, the chairman of the board, called a big shop meeting for all the employees. At the end of his speech he said to us that there is nobody in this shop that is too **big** to help the

littlest guy. Just after that pep talk I was carrying a load of valves down the hallway and I saw Mr. Crawford coming along with six guys walking behind him. I was just a young smart aleck so I said, "Hey, Fred, give me a hand with these valves." He said, "Sure." Those six guys were like to fall dead when they saw the two of us pushing the dolly of valves down the hallway. People on both sides see us walking together, talking together. Fred Crawford is asking me how long I've been with the Company, how much money I got saved. He says he likes his employees that way.

He never forgot me. Whenever he came into the plant he'd say, "Hey, Jess — come over here." Those guys under him who saw us together must have thought I was Crawford's boy — that I must have been his yardboy or his caddy, or something. That kind of greased the skids for me at Thompson Products and I went right on up. But after the war when they started closing down part of the plant for retooling I didn't want to be transferred way out to their Tapco Division, so I got laid off.

That's when I went down to City Hall and I said I was ready to work for the City. This was 1947. The civil service officer said he was going to send me to the West Side Market because blacks hadn't been able to stay there, and he wanted me to report back to him what was going on at the Market. But when I came over here, everybody treated me all right; maybe they were tipped off that I was going to report on them. Tom Daley, the superintendent of the Market, took me into the saloon where no colored were seen, and he told all the guys, "This man works for me, you treat him just like everyone else."

I started in as an engineer's man, learning everything about the place. One day, Thompson Products called me back to work. The Commissioner took the call in his office and when I came in to answer the phone, he put his hand over the receiver and whispered, "Don't leave me — I've got something good for you in the Market." I grow on people easy, I guess. Anyhow, I figured maybe Thompson Products would lay me off again if I went back to them so I thought I'd give the Market a chance. The Commissioner said, "Wear your suit tomorrow." The next day two sealers (guys who check all the weights and measures) took me out with them. They only took me where they had free coffee and free sandwiches, no work! It was all put up between the Commissioner and them. I said to myself: I'm getting a job like **this!** They kept promising me, but that job never came up.

Meanwhile I worked as an extra man, covering for people nights, holidays, working everywhere in the Market. I worked a lot here on the dock. Up until the big renovation in 1954 the dock was run on a short-term storage system. Every time an outside vendor brought something in to store he had to pay for it: 12 cents a bushel, 8 cents a box. The merchandise had to be put on the dock and our men would carry it downstairs. Florida oranges came packed in crates made out of wood. Heavy! They weighed like the devil. Carrots, lettuce were weighted down with ice. Today it's all much easier to handle.

I been here over 35 years; I'm foreman of the Market. All the same problems were mine long before I had the title. You know, this is the best market in the whole world. I like the building. I like everything about it. It's an **intimate** place. The inside and outside, they're from two different worlds. All the merchants, I knew their **fathers.** The old timers outside, the "Dons" I called them, they were tough. Mostly Italian. The old man would run the show. In the outside stands they're all intermarried. There are cousins all over the place! Annie Palmisano, her mother is Mrs. O'Toole. "Big Louie" Rolofsky, he married that Italian girl. Old Man Schilla was one of the original "Dons." His wife once told me, "When I married Charlie he warned me not to have any babies on Friday or Saturday — because those days I had to help in the Market. And here he goes and dies on a Friday!"

From my place here on the dock, I've seen it all. I'm going to tell you about that lady you always see out there picking out of the garbage cans, that thin lady with the little dog. She's from a well-to-do family; she left, wandered away from home or something. She sleeps under the bridge over there. Her family finally located her here; her husband came and found her picking in the garbage. He said, "You don't have to pick in no garbage!" He went inside and bought some prime steaks and brought them out to her. She took those steaks and threw them in the garbage and she kept right on picking out of the bins. He took her home and they cleaned her up, dressed her up, got her hair done. They kept her away for quite awhile. All of a sudden, she was right back.

I'll tell you another one. There was an old lady and she had a little dog, too. She used to sit out here all the time in the summertime. She had her place — you know the regulars, these bums, they each have their place. She died. She left two houses that sat on one lot, right over where the parking lot for the Market is now. She had two daughters. They moved in a house apiece. Because the houses sat on the one lot, there was only one tax to be paid. So, you know what? This daughter wouldn't pay it, the other daughter wouldn't pay it. You know what happened? The City auctioned off those houses for the taxes owed. The Market Association bought those two houses for 10,000 dollars and tore them down to build the new parking lot. See how people can be.

There's another guy around here. He had a little problem. He was foreman in a steel mill, his father was foreman before him. He happened to come home one day and he found some guy with his wife. So, for nine months he never went back to work, he never went **home** again. He was the best-dressed bum around here. Just drinking and hanging around here. I guess his wife got a divorce and took the house, everything.

He had an uncle who I thought was a straight-out bum. This uncle brought shopping bags around here, three-in-one shopping bags. He'd sit right there near the dock and wait until something came out in the garbage. If I happened to push a truck out, I'd tell him, "That one's heavy, maybe there's something good in there." He died. It turned out that he owned four houses over on Jay Avenue and he had 27,000 dollars in the bank. He willed it all to his nephew, the bum whose wife took everything and moved to California with his four kids.

That guy put all that inheritance in the bank; I know because he showed me all the papers. He has never changed his ways; he lives right across the street in that building there. He sold the houses and the 27,000 dollars came up to 57,000 dollars; he showed me the bankbook. These guys think he's just a bum. I tell them he's the richest bum around. He showed me some letters he got from California from his kids. They heard about his big inheritance and they said, "Come out here and you and Ma can get back together!"

Oh yeah, I've seen plenty. At one time, when I first came here, if you wanted a job done there was a guy lying around here who could do it. There were machinists, there were electricians, there were plumbers. Guys drunk all day long, not working, not doing anything. I mean, they had a trade — they weren't dummies. One guy was a contractor. One guy, I don't know what he was, but his mother brought him a clean suit of clothes every week, clean shirt and everything. He changed right in the toilet. By the next week he was so black and dirty, she brought him a new one.

They live outside, sleep around various places. These guys were good. And they knew me, too, because they found out quick that I had a bus pass from the City at that time (they didn't give me a car!). They borrowed my bus pass and they'd ride out to 98th and Lorain somewhere further out to get a bottle of bay rum; the drugstores around here wouldn't sell it to them because they knew they were going to make whiskey. They'd get the rum and a can of pineapple juice and mix it all together.

They were honest people, they didn't take anything. They were just that way. Something happened to them in life, you know. Something happened — and changed their perspective.

SOMMER BROTHERS

From the day Sommer's Meats opened for business in 1914, Arnold Sommer remained a key figure in the Market until his death at the age of 84, about six years ago. His sons, Edgar and Leonard, continue the congenial family partnership they have enjoyed for most of their adult lives.

The tall, intent man behind the counter is Edgar, the older brother. He runs the business up here in the Markethouse, dealing with the public, doing all the selling and merchandising. He hugs the receiver between his shoulder and his ear, talking quickly. The other end of the inter-com phone is answered down in the cooler by his brother, Leonard. Rosy-cheeked and affable, Leonard sets to work cutting the order for veal scallopini that Edgar has just called down. He does all the buying and cutting of the meat, remaining year-round in the subterranean climate of 36 degrees Fahrenheit.

For 35 years, the two Sommer brothers have been holding down opposite ends of the teeter-totter, balancing the family business between them. Edgar, close to 70, straddles the upper end; Leonard, just a couple of years younger, grips the bottom with his strong hands. Each holds the other in balance; they can't get along one without the other.

LEONARD: They say that a business partnership among family is bad. But my father, my brother Edgar and I got along very well for 35 years. I've enjoyed our business, our working together.

EDGAR: Grandfather was a baker in a small town near Bern, Switzerland. He wanted to try his luck in the world, so in 1887 he came to Cleveland where friends found him a job with the old Cleveland Baking Company. Within a year he had saved enough to send for his wife and three children. Our dad was the youngest of the three.

My grandmother often described her surprise upon arriving at Ellis Island. There were fireworks in the harbor and small boats shooting off streams of water and she thought to herself: how wonderful that immigrants are welcomed this way in America! Later she found out it was the Fourth of July, 1888. She marveled that the train carrying them to Cleveland had green upholstered seats in the coaches, while in Europe she had to sit on wooden benches. When they arrived at the old Union Station, my grandfather was there to greet his family after their year's separation and he spoke to them in English! My grandmother was mortified. Grandfather was just trying to show off, but this was how he made them understand that this was his adopted country and English was the language they would speak. The family was permitted to speak the Swiss-German dialect only at the dinner table.

LEONARD: As the family grew, our dad had to leave school to help support his brothers and sisters so he began working at John Koenigshoff's butcher stand in the old Central Market. The day my dad got his own stand here at the West Side Market was the day I was born in 1914.

EDGAR: At one point during the Depression,

Leonard Sommer.

when things were rough down here, I was thinking to myself that there had to be something else to life. One of our customers owned Fogel Lithography and he offered me the chance to come to work as a printer's apprentice. That's where I got the biggest surprise. As a printer I was working with chemicals and film. That stuff didn't spoil like meat would spoil and at first I thought that was great. But after about two years, I just wanted to get back to this world of the Market where things **spoiled.** It's in your blood, I guess.

LEONARD: So, we've been in this together a long time now. I do the buying and the cutting

down in the cooler and Edgar runs the business upstairs at the counter.

EDGAR: We learned the business just by growing up around it. All my dad's grandchildren have had an apron on at one time or another.

LEONARD: I used to look at every piece of meat before I bought it; every morning I went to the slaughterhouse. A hundred cattle could be killed and they'd all be marked "choice," but there'd be maybe 10 or 12 that I would want. Meat grows. It's not manufactured and there's a reason for some meat being better: the breed, the conformation, the age. But now you won't see white-faced Herefords, Angus cattle any-

179

Edgar Sommer.

more; they're cross-breeding to get the bigger size in the younger animal. The local slaughter-houses are closed; I buy my veal and lamb from Detroit Packing. I can't look at it anymore. I have to put myself in the hands of a salesman at the other end of a long distance telephone and I just have to hope that he realizes who I am.

EDGAR: We open our stand at seven in the morning but some old-timers come through the loading dock doors before the Market opens. Fridays and Saturdays we have a pretty good business even before we turn the lights on. It's a throwback to the days when people thought that if they got there early, they were gonna get the best.

LEONARD: Veal and lamb are very high now and since the chain stores don't carry too much of it, that makes it better for us. At seven-thirty in

the morning my daughter Christine will tell a customer that we're all out of veal steak. The customer will complain, "My God! What happened?" Christine will explain that it's almost five dollars a pound and we don't cut too much. The woman who wants it is there early and she'll lecture us, "I didn't ask you how much it costs — I want it! You save me five pounds of veal for next Saturday — for sure!"

Some of these old-timers still live on the South Side. Their house has been paid for for 50 years; they don't want a new car — they don't even want a vacation. Their husbands work in the steel mill and make a good dollar. They remember when they didn't have any money to buy meat, then they remember when they had the money and couldn't get any meat. So now when they want something, they yell.

"I remember clearly when
the Markethouse opened
in 1912; there was an eclipse
of the sun that year."

DR. THEO NYERGES

Like Merlin the Wizard charting the constellations to his own design, Theo Nyerges, Doctor of Dental Surgery, takes the measure of the Markethouse, squinting down from his small office window above Market Square. Waving his wand, which glints suspiciously like a metal dental mirror, he reverses time to travel back through the light-years to his childhood in this neighborhood. Theo filters the early scenes through a magical filigrée spun from strands of dental floss and colorful memory.

Through the flashing prism of his keen eye he focuses on particular moments in the early development of the near West Side. The decades brush past Dr. Nyerges, barely marking him; it has been more than 40 years now that his offices have been located up in the United Bank Building across the street from the Market. He paces about the cramped consultation room, soldering the star-spangled stories of his personal life onto fantastic cosmic events.

I remember when they were excavating the hole for the West Side Markethouse. They were using work horses and wagons to clear out the pit. I was a tiny kid on my way home from my aunt's house and I sneaked into that big hole and I caught a sparrow, bare-handed. It squeaked so loud I let it go.

I was born in 1906 at 1901 Lorain, which is where the Lorain-Carnegie bridge abutment begins now. The street is still there, but about the turn of the century they changed the names to numbers. Our street was in a dead end called the Grove, an overhang that didn't lead anywhere. The way across to the east side was the Abbey Street bridge and then the Central Viaduct.

I remember the old Markethouse, it was the same structure as the old Central Market — a flat one-story building and it was full of butchers, vendors — and I think it was a rat haven. The blacksmiths' shops stunk from steaming leather, the horses with red-hot shoes on them. They used to do the shoeing in the back. Lorain Avenue, what was it like? Well, before my time every other store along Lorain was a saloon. But it was also a city of churches. They were burning kerosene lamps all the way over from Franklin to Munroe; in those days it was dirtier than hell.

Firestation Number Six was located on the triangle between the Bridge and the Markethouse. I remember they had a beautiful horse-drawn Peerless fire truck. Three horses pulled that big steamer; it used to go clang-clang-clang and in a few seconds they were off. The firehouse was built on a slight mound, kind of like a turtle shell, so they pushed the wagon down the incline and the horses had no trouble pulling the steamer. I used to hang around and watch the horses drink out of the big watering trough; the dogs would

Theo Nyerges
still swears
by his
55-year-old
X-ray machine.

drink out of it, too. They were humane about dogs then.

We moved from this neighborhood in 1910, when Halley's Comet passed over. I know I saw it, but I don't remember because I was only four years old. What I do remember is that my older brothers went up the back steps to see the comet and one of them fell down the steps and saw Saturn instead! We didn't really leave this neighborhood; we moved two miles away to West 47th Street.

This was the strip, between Bridge Avenue and Lorain; it was the original shopping mall and any good store worthy of having was here. Everyone went to Fries and Schuele's or John Meckes' Department Store and the Dime Store. Frank X. Russert the Jeweler and Sommers the Umbrella Man — they shared the same store. Manuel's Candies is still there. And then there was Expolis, a good Greek name, the candy kitchen. I worked for him for a short time but I was eating him out of house and home.

Then they opened the West Side Market. What a marvelous thing. Saturday nights we

183

Horse-drawn
fire engine
leaving old
Fire Station Six.

kids at home couldn't wait until our mother got back from the Market because she'd bring some goodies. I remember clearly when the Markethouse opened in 1912; there was an eclipse of the sun that year. These natural events are interesting to recall because they verify dates.

This was like a little Downtown. There were some of the finest theaters around here. The Majestic, which competed with the downtown theaters had a stage that was second to none. When they built the Lorain-Carnegie bridge in 1932 times were so bad that it was almost a useless bridge. They built it as a double-decker so that streetcars could run under it, but they didn't. It was the Depression. I remember the junk and rag peddlers would cross the bridge in their wagons on their trip back home to the East Side.

As I was growing up I didn't know what the hell I wanted to be. I was small, I was clever; I wasn't a genius but I could hammer something together and it looked all right. My brother said, "You've got hands like a monkey." I was going to be a ball player or a pitcher. Somebody said, "Wouldn't you like to be a doctor?" Because they dress well.

My brother went to Case College and he was on the track team. Being a kid, I wanted to do the same thing. Well, I was 42 out of a list of 55 in grades — that's low! I never studied in my life; I've never had to. I went and took the Case entrance examinations. I didn't study; Jesus, I failed them all. But in the I.Q. test my name was on the top of the list! I wasn't surprised but I was elated. Reserve was having their examinations a week later so I decided to try them. I was on the streetcar riding out to Reserve to take the exams when I met a friend of the family. He asked, "Where are you going, kid?" I told him that I had really wanted to go to Case and be an engineer but now I was going to try for Reserve. He said, "Oh, hell, you don't want to be an engineer. Be a dentist or something like that." Well, it rang a bell.

I went to Reserve. As freshmen we had to wear little beanie caps when we left chapel or else we had to dance around a pole. Well, those beanie caps cost 75 cents and somebody stole mine. I was afraid to go to chapel without it and I decided the hell with the dancing. So, I didn't attend and I got kicked out of school for flunking chapel. But, I've been lucky all my life. I intercepted the letter announcing my dismissal from Reserve and hid it somewhere until my mother went on a trip to see my grandmother before she died. I had already registered for summer school so I went just as if nothing was wrong. I took industrial chemistry and I really enjoyed it. We just took rides all over and went through every big factory in town. September rolled around and I received a notice saying, "You are hereby reinstated." See, they didn't know what they were doing.

I graduated from Western Reserve Dental School in 1928 and here I am still practicing dentistry 53 years later. I think I could have done just about anything with my life. I don't think I would have ever become an opera singer because I never had the voice — but I could have been an insurance man, a salesman. As a young dentist it took me quite a while to settle down. I was still single when I was 30 years old and people would ask me why do married men live longer than single men? I told them, "They don't. It just **seems** longer!"

I've been up here in my office looking down on Market Square for over 40 years now. I know a lot of the merchants in the Market — many of them are my patients over a lifetime. I know the Stumpfs, the Ehrnfelts, Walter Simmelink. I'm within a stone's throw of where I was born and the Market and I are still carrying on. I'm 75 years old and I **feel** it sometimes. I feel like a hundred. I've got asthma; I smoked Camels for 50 years and I wouldn't change to filters because someday I knew I could quit Camels — and I did. Ten years it's been now and I wouldn't smoke with a gun to my head. My bones hurt like hell, but I can't retire.

Early scenes
at the
West Side Market.

"... fresh vegetables
will be a thing of the past.
You'll be eating artificial stuff."

NORMAN DILL

Ask any outdoor vendor for an off-beat item and he's sure to send you straight over to Norman Dill. On the spur off to the left of the main arcade, the space opens up behind the stands and Norman can back his truck directly up to his stall and unload the variety of homegrown produce he has collected. The Dills themselves once were growers as well as vendors, but he has long since given up the greenhouses for lack of adequate help.

    Norman Dill still clings to the old-fashioned notion that food should be homegrown. Because most of the small farmers are being forced out of existence, he has improvised his own solution to the problem. Like Johnny Appleseed, he takes seed to retired farmers he knows and instructs them to raise special fruits and vegetables for him. He then rides his circuit collecting this produce and offers it for sale in his Market stand. In his own stubborn way, Norman is protecting two endangered species: the small truck gardener and the exotic fruits and vegetables. He doesn't see himself in this role of conservationist; he's just a hardworking guy, trying to make an honest buck.

WHY do I hang around the Market? I'm used to it. I've been my own boss all my life. Trouble is, if you go to work for somebody after you've been your own boss, you kill the job. You push like crazy until it's done, before you ever sit down, while the other ones loaf along, stretch a job out. From the day I was born, from what I hear, my mother and father would bring me down here to take care of me; they put me in a wash basket under the stand. My folks got the stand in 1918 when they got married. My father had a heart attack when I was 17 so then it was my mother and me. From then on I was more or less running the stand. My father actually turned it over to me on the first of April, 1956, and on the 11th he died. My mother died 18 months later. They'd worked together all their life. When one went, that was it. Well, in 1918 when they first got married they had that double flu, pneumonia; that might have weakened them.

    I been here too long. I know 'em all. The ones who are the regular customers, I know what they're going to do when they step up in front of the counter. I don't know any by name, only by face. I got one, must be an Irishman, he wants yellow cucumbers to make pickles. Oh, I get hot once in a while, like when people come up to my stand and they want a deal when they buy one basket. They say, "How much you going to give me off if I buy two?" I say, "The same as you get off in a gas station when you fill up." The worse the economy gets, the more they come down here looking for cheaper stuff. Where else can a person go and grumble to the guy you're buying from? Most people don't know what's good or bad — they buy by price. Like I tell 'em, "You've been eating all your life and you know the **least** thing about it. The thing

you do the most of, you know the least about. They never knew what good stuff was. The good customers aren't like that.

This time of year I've got a lot of them looking for local stuff. Like this morning, they're looking for cucumbers without wax. All your shipped stuff is waxed. We don't want to wax it; we want to sell it. Oh yeah, the other merchants know that if the customers ask them for stuff they don't have they should send them down to me. If they ask for **weird** stuff, they send them **all** down to me. They say if he hasn't got it, you aren't going to find it.

See, most vendors don't want to do the chasing to get special items. I've got 10 or 12 guys growing especially for me. I tell them what I want and they raise it. I got to know these local farmers when we used to run short and we'd buy from them. Then, when they quit doing farming, they still wanted to monkey around with a garden so I tell them what I want and they raise it. Yep, these farmers are retired, two of them are in their 80s. It gives them something to look forward to. See, if they only have a little bit of garden these big buyers won't deal with them. I go as far as Sandusky to pick up from them; my route round-trip is just under 100 miles. I pick up on Tuesdays and Thursdays or they bring whatever they've got for me on Friday nights. So, this way they get a little spending money for the summertime and I get all fresh.

I can offer my customers stuff that nobody else would bother with. Gooseberries, currants. Sour cherries — I handle a lot of them. I was the first one to have them in Cleveland, I think. I've got two orchards west of here I work out of. I carry Chinese winter melons. My Chinese customers got me the seed and I gave it to one of my growers and he grows it for me. I handle herbs: basil, coriander, sage, marjoram — fresh. I'm willing to try out anything. One wintertime I had nothing to sell. I saw someone down here handling peanuts and I said I'm going to try it. Everyone thought I was nuts. I sold 100 pounds of unshelled peanuts in a week; I think that's a pretty good deal. I've got one customer now who buys nine pounds a week; she's feeding birds. Three pounds of peanuts each Market day. She comes with a cart, she walks it in the summertime.

I don't plan on nothing. Just take it as it comes, that's all. Start out the first of the year, you're running apples from the year before. Get up to Easter, you've got the Easter plants, then you start bedding plants, then your homegrown stuff. When I was younger and still growing stuff in my own greenhouse I was crazy enough to try anything — spaghetti squash, we've been handling that for 30 years. It's not a new item, it just hadn't been publicized, that's all.

In not too many years, fresh vegetables will be a thing of the past. You'll be eating artificial stuff. Yeah, it's scary. Right now, everybody's complaining they can't get any pickers. One friend of mine has seven or eight acres of blueberries — can't get nobody to pick 'em for him. They want a big buck and they don't want to do nothing. You stay out there in the sun and that's no fun. So, the small farmers are quitting; they can't make it.

Well, most of your garden land is being chewed up for developments. Avon used to be a big farming area and there are very few farms there now. So, you've got 25-30 acres and you get up to 60 years old and you sell it off — you can live off what you got for your land. The sons can't take over because the operating expenses are too high. Growing produce is tough.

They can't afford to grow it because they can't get their price out of it. The young people won't take it on. A guy told me that the only time you get anything out of your kids is from 14 to 16, and forget it after they're 16 because they get too expensive. A car they want, all this stuff. They won't take and fight for a little dollar like we used to.

So pretty soon now we'll be eating artificial food. You want to hear something good? A lady friend of mine wants to buy a toy for one of her grandchildren who has a birthday coming up. She wants to buy him one of those little toy sets of farm animals. She's been looking around and she says, "I don't want a green cow and a purple pig! I want natural colors." But she told me she can't find them anywhere. Nothing natural no more. She had tears in her eyes.

Down here at the Market they tell me, "As long as you grumble, you're happy." I'll tell you, I'd be a lot happier if I had some time to myself. I didn't go square dancing until three years ago, after my wife died. My sister said, "We're going to take square dance lessons." I didn't think much of it. Now I can go three, four nights a week. But, I've got all these old guys, these retired farmers growing stuff for me, how can I take off and leave them sitting?

It's just me, more or less, running this whole deal. Once in a while on a Saturday my older son can help me. If I get real tight, my sister helps. And I got this kid who's working for me, his grandfather comes and helps. He used to be a produce man in one of the chain stores. He loves it here. Did I ever think of doing anything else? I didn't have time. I threatened to get out a lot of times — hell, where am I gonna go?

For several years before the restoration project in Ohio City took hold, there had been a rash of fires set by vandals, incinerating the unused buildings and boarded-up houses. On a block of West 28th Street the razing of gutted hulls has left one small brick building standing alone in a landscape reminiscent of the London Blitz.

Nailed to the door of the lone building is a wooden sign: FARKAS PASTRY SHOP. The solid door shields a dessert lover's paradise from the prevailing desolation. Inside, the plain room gives no hint of hedonism. Two large institutional coolers line one wall, two metal pastry carts stand empty in the middle of the room. A wooden shelf over the steel worktable accomodates a ball of string, a scotch tape dispenser and a pile of flattened white boxes. The only decoration on the walls is the license issued by the Department of Health.

Stepping gracefully into the center of the austere space is a handsome, intensely alert man dressed in a white golf shirt and white pants. Moving quickly, with the haughty assurance of a matador, Attila Farkas approaches the table and plunges his knife cleanly through the six-inch custard of a Napolean cream square, impaling a quivering sample on the blade's point. Over the years, Attila's brash arrogance has mellowed into a good-humored pride; he KNOWS he is wonderful!

With an elegant sweep he pulls open the large cooler door to reveal a dense lava flow of pink icings, molten chocolates. He lifts out a glistening torte which appears more voluptuous in the sterile room; he lowers it into a box, ties it neatly with a string. In the alcove beyond the room stand the few tools of his trade: an enormous pizza oven, a restaurant cooler, an institutional mixer. From his outpost in the midst of the devastated neighborhood, Attila, the optimistic survivor, cheerfully confirms that things are getting better around here.

"I would say anyone who recognizes quality would CARE. I mean, there is no way not to recognize the difference between vegetable oil and sweet butter."

ATTILA FARKAS

I'M named for our great forefather, Attila the Hun. Two tribes were traveling together from the east and when they separated, Attila took his Huns and terrorized the world for a while. Then he got a nosebleed and died. He was a rough, tough guy. I don't want to talk politics, but Hungary has had its share of rough guys more recently, which is why I am here today. When the Communists "nationalized" our family's pastry business, they came in one day and said, "Give us the keys." And out we went. They took over, plain and simple — no financial remuneration, nothing. That was January 13, 1950.

My father had one of the finest pastry shops in Hungary, right smack in downtown Budapest. It was one of those large sidewalk cafes that are so famous in Hungary, with espresso and demitasse served under the awnings. He had 15 employees and a great set-up that was worth over a quarter of a million dollars just in machinery and property. The place was loaded with the greatest refrigeration systems and mixers — you name it. He used to go to the international fairs in Germany and buy the most modern equipment; even back in 1940 he had the best washing and drying machines in the world.

I was still going to school when they took over the business. At that time, the Communists were really leaning on anybody who had had anything beforehand. So, although I graduated with honors in school, for political reasons they did not accept me at the University. They were punishing me for my father's sin of having had a successful business, which he had struggled very hard to build up from nothing. When I was born the times were too turbulent — Hitler was getting ready, the Second World War was just about starting, so my parents figured they weren't

going to bring any more children into this world. So, I'm the only child.

In 1956 after the Revolution, my dad and I came out alone as pioneers; we had to leave my mother and grandmother behind. All the Hungarian refugees, "freedom fighters" as we were called, came to Camp Kilmer in New Jersey. The Americans who wanted to sponsor these people or offer them jobs were calling and coming to the Camp. We met an American businessman who was willing to back us in the bakery business in a small town in Maryland where they didn't have a decent loaf of bread. So, we tried to set up an American-style pastry business.

When we arrived, I could not speak a word of English but because of my love of sports I found a way to learn the language. I had never seen a TV set in my life, and so I was fascinated and watched the Baltimore Orioles play baseball on TV; I fell in love with them. I stayed up until 11, 12 every single summer night listening to the Orioles' night games broadcast on the radio. The announcers spoke so beautifully that I could understand. It was the strangest way to learn English; I learned "bunt" and "home run" and "triple" before I learned anything else.

We soon realized that the American bakery business was not our bag. We were not very happy, so we worked to pay off all our debts to the man and when we left that town in Maryland after a year, we were absolutely clean. We had friends who had come out at the same time with us who were in Cleveland; for two generations this was already known as a big Hungarian town. About 60,000 refugees came here because it is a big industrial town with plenty of work available. We came here on a Saturday in 1959 and I was working on Monday. My father went to work for Kaase's Bakeries. They were a Dutch family chain with 104 stores when he started working for them.

Mom finally made her appearance here in 1965; diplomatic relationships between Hungary and the States had sort of warmed up by then. For all those years it had been impossible to move back and forth. When Mom came, she compelled us to start our own business. Dad's talents had been wasted for seven years at Kaase's but his primary concern had been to make a living. We set up right here, where we still are today. January 1, 1966, was when we opened. The word spread very quickly. Hungarians love good food and when our pastries first came out, I mean, it went like **wildfire** and it has just burned on and on. I haven't spent one dollar on advertising yet!

Being a one-man operation is strictly my

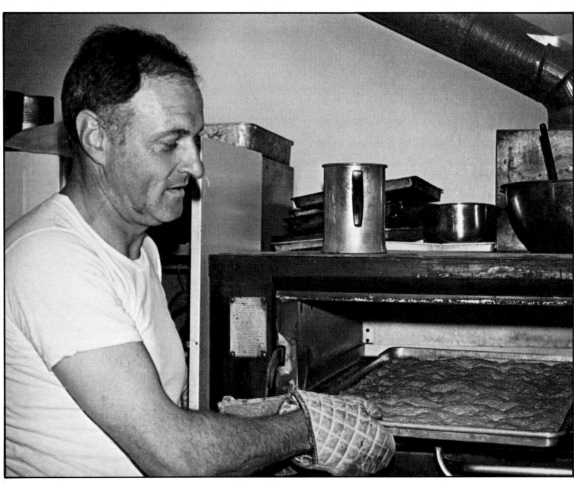

own choosing. I could have done many different things with the business, but I am comfortable with doing what I want to do, and I couldn't care less what other people say. Let them live their life and leave me alone. Once you get this feeling that your father was a man of his own, then you're a man of your own — I don't think you can go through the transition.

If I'm not proud of the product, I won't make it. I'd rather settle for less profits, but I won't compromise my recipes. If they would price me out with the rising cost of the best ingredients, I would have to go out of business because I refuse to make garbage. That's a legend coming down from my father — it's not my own making. All the credit is due him for my attitude. I would say anyone who recognizes quality would **care**! I mean, there is no way not to recognize the difference between vegetable oil and sweet butter.

The butter I use happens to be the highest grade, 92 score, which is the best in the country. I get my butter from Walter Simmelink at the West Side Market; Simmelink doesn't deal with garbage, either. I buy my sweet butter from him in the hugest quantity available: one block of sweet butter is 68 pounds. Depending on business, I buy one, sometimes two blocks a week from him. I think I use more sweet butter than anybody else in town — you can put that in the records!

I think the people in the Market are marvelous because they're their own people. Nobody is commanding them. Without the Market, I think there was a time when this area would have gone down the drain — right down the Cuyahoga River. I weathered those hard times around here because I started to think, it should start to turn to the better, so why should I jump somewhere else? And it definitely has. Because of the fine restaurants and establishments that have come in here, the area has become not only better but more interesting.

One of my reasons for staying around this area is the drawing power of the Market. I do have a lot of people, who, when they visit the Market, they visit me. It's a **must** when they go to the Market; they go to Farkas the Sausage Man and then they come over here to Farkas the Pastry Man. Although a large part of my business is wholesale to restaurants and clubs, I'm always open to the public on Fridays and Saturdays. I love those days; my personality's suitable to being around a lot of people and I like to talk with them. Strange as it sounds, this little hole-in-the-wall attracts an amazing conglomeration of people. I have from lawyers and mayors to drunks and derelicts. So, I have a good range.

My dad is 78 years old although he looks 60; they call him the Baron. He retired about four years ago but when he's around here he's got to have his hands in. His hands, yes, his hands are still the fastest I've ever seen. Nobody in this business is as fast as he is. He was very, very innovative in a business that is very much steeped in the tradition of hundreds and hundreds of years — you don't change a Doboschtorte! Yet, Dad was able to come up with new things; he is famous for his innovation of the "corner house." He took a slice of torte and built it up all around with whipped cream; everybody in Hungary knows what a corner house is.

I think our first trip back to Hungary was in 1968. By then the pioneers had gone to scout the area and when they came back, unharmed, we finally decided to go home. We have gone back frequently since then. It was a nostalgic and hard time for Dad to go back to see his pastry shop. It is still an excellent shop in the heart of Budapest; the state runs it, everything is there in the same place. Dad sits around in the sidewalk cafe under the awnings and when a young waiter comes to serve him, he grabs him by the sleeve and tells him, "You know, I used to own this." He can't let anyone go by without telling it.

The name EHRNFELT first reverberated off the tile walls of the Markethouse on opening day in 1912. It has been called out over four generations, touting the Ehrnfelt specialty: beef. Great-Grandfather Gottleib and Grandfather Walter, Sr., knew no other life. Walter, Jr., next in the line, grew up in the business, raised his family and became interested in politics. When he recently won election as Mayor of the nearby city of Strongsville, the responsibility for Ehrnfelt Meats was passed on to his son, Wally III.

If Great-Grandfather and Grandfather were alive today, they could stand close with the two younger men to form a great butchershop quartet. Voices blending in four-part harmony, they would sing together the ballad of all the families who have made the Market their life's work. The special lyric croons for all of them, both of them, each of them:

> Do like my father did —
> Learned it all as a kid.
> TIME is the price I pay —
> The prize is life my way.

"I was never, EVER going to do that — be a butcher." Walter II Wally III

THE EHRNFELT FAMILY

WALTER II: People today have not accepted the computer as the total way to shop. We are four generations of Ehrnfelts in the Market, and I feel very optimistic. I did hate to see Fries and Schuele Department Store go. The main reason they went out was that those fellows were getting up in years and the sons and daughters just weren't interested in the business. That's how a lot of these businesses die. But so far, the Ehrnfelts have kept the enthusiasm. Of course, I used to gripe about it a little bit, when I was a kid, and of course, I was never, **ever** going to do that — be a butcher. It's something that kind of grows on you.

WALLY III: I guess basically, I've been doing this since I was a little kid, same way my dad did. He'd bring me down here from about the time I was eight; I would work on the weekends.

WALTER II: In the early days, if you were **big** enough, you were **old** enough! I started out with everything by hand. We didn't have electric saws. We got the cattle in four big pieces and processed it from there. That's why sometimes people ask me why I have big arms. Even though I was an athlete and had to play basketball and football on Friday nights, I was expected to be here on Saturday morning to work. A lot of times I would be given a little grace and not get here until seven A.M.

WALLY III: I figured the meat business was too hard for me. I wanted to get something where I could make a lot of money and not have to work hard. I went away to Wittenberg University and majored in political science. When I graduated, I thought about going on to law school.

WALTER II: It was funny, when Wally graduated from college, I said, "I haven't had a real vacation in 20 years, so you have to come and work for at least three months." Then I went on

Wally III and his
mother,
guarded by the
longhorn steer.

Walter Ehrnfelt,
Senior,
astride his famous
"golden bull."

my fishing trip to Alaska. And he's been here ever since.

WALLY III: What it came down to, was I wanted to pay my father back for all the years he worked his tail off to put me through school so that I could do the things I wanted to do. And I thought that the best way that I could sort of start paying my debt to him was to let him have some **time** to pursue some of the things he'd like to do. And it turned out that politics was one of them. He ran for office last November and I'm proud to announce that he won a four-year term as Mayor of Strongsville. So, if you want to catch my dad, you'll have to call City Hall.

WALTER II: I have always been fairly active on the Board of Directors of the Market Tenants' Association; my father was on the Board before me. I served as president for nine years. We really play a very important role for the Market as a whole. We have nine directors elected by the tenants, and then we choose our officers.

WALLY III: My father served as president of the Association and now I'm the president. We've got sort of a young crowd that's becoming

The mayor of Strongsville lends a hand.

interested in the Market concept. Like any other situation, you have to establish your credibility with the old-timers. You have to make them know that you're on the same level as they are, in the same business. That's probably the hardest part. But once you get past that point, everybody realizes that we're all in this together. We're independent but our cause is the West Side Market. I haven't really had any problem with the generation gap, so to speak.

My best experience in the Market has been that I've learned that what we have is a small scale of any business. I get involved here in all aspects — the purchasing, the selling, the production, and it's really good knowledge. A lot of

guys my age get lost in those corporate structures where they have no idea what's involved in another department. I have had to realize what it takes from start to finish and all aspects in between. I think that knowledge has been really good for me.

WALTER II: I have customers here who dealt with my grandfather — and he died in 1937! I can remember my dad telling stories about what went on in this place in the old days. If a guy would walk in the Market with a white shirt and tie on, somebody would throw a piece of liver at him. Bring him down a peg or two.

WALLY III: This place is just so unique and interesting but it demands a big dedication. People are shopping here at five in the morning and you have to be here. I enjoy the physical labor, the crazy hours — it's all part of the life. I had to take a strong line; it's a situation where if you wanted to think about what you're making per hour, it would drive you crazy.

WALTER II: Everybody asks about the steer's head we have mounted over our stand. That's an educational item, a longhorn steer, and that goes way back. It came off the big King Ranch in Texas. To get that big it would have to be about 25 years old. The longhorns are pretty much a lost breed because they're long and rangy, bony, and they don't put on weight very well. They were durable, though, and mean — they'd fight off the wolves. They could withstand drought and intense heat and cold. When the King Ranch switched to mixed breeds, the Herefords, the Brahmas, they had to keep a few of these old bulls on the property; they were known as "lead" bulls because they knew where the water-holes were and could lead the new cattle to those watering spots.

WALLY III: Every once in a while people come through asking for the weirdest things. I had some people, I think they were Chinese, requesting the cow's feet, hooves and all with the hair on them and everything. I got some in from the packing house, they still had manure all over them. That's what they wanted — to make soup. Another guy, Mexican guy, wanted the whole cow's head. I asked what he does with it. "Oh, you put it on a rotisserie; it's great that way!"

WALTER II: Every year at Christmas time there is a German band that comes to serenade the customers; they set up on the balcony and play all the favorite music from the Old Country. You know, I have had this happen many times throughout the years, you'll be waiting on a lady at your counter and they'll start to play "O Tannenbaum" and the tears will just be rolling down her face. It's very touching. The vendors have been seen wiping their eyes, too.

WALLY III: The inter-relationships with people in here is something we just **can't** let go. We've got to keep it going. We also have a strong family situation and we all try to help each other.

My mother comes in on Thursdays to help me wrap freezer orders. Up until a few months ago, my grandmother had been working steady, but her bursitis started acting up. My sister Susan has a family of her own, but she helps me on Friday. She just likes to come down here and be involved. When she was younger, we just couldn't drag Susan down here; all of a sudden she was sure to get a real bad headache. But as we get older, we've come to love this place.

WALTER II: Occasionally now I still work a Saturday, but Wally runs the place. If I have a meeting in the area and I'm breezing by, why, I stop at the Market for a minute.

WALLY III: My daughter is six years old; my son is three. I've had my little girl down here on Thursdays a few times already, helping me work. She likes to push the buttons on the cash register.

Wally III, assisted by his younger brother, Bobby.

Members of the West Side Market Tenants' Association proudly pose in front of
their Markethouse (above, 1915; below left, 1937).

...ION AND EMPLOYEES ~~~~~~ CLEVELAND, OHIO
FEB. 20, 1915.

BY THE MILLER STUDIO
2208 CLARK AVE.

The West Side Market; a fine place for meeting friends. The market place as meeting place.

EPILOGUE

*. . . My stomach growled as I walked through the Market. I wanted some of everything. I had some strawberries and oranges. They were the best fruit I have ever tasted.

*. . . Being a kid is an advantage because you get discounts. One of the good things about the Market is that you can just look around as long as you want and nobody gets impatient.

*VOICES OF CHILDREN, OVERHEARD IN THE MARKET . . .

All the story-telling! The Market people chanting in unison, then in solo voice — all, each repeating the refrain: IT GETS IN YOUR BLOOD. The pulse of family, of village; the stirring of person to person; the heat of competition; the rhythm of daily work. When Mary Tricsko says, "Once you step inside, you get this incurable Market fever," and Henry Pawlowski says, "If it was open on Sunday, I'd come down here on Sunday," what are they saying?

The Markethouse for generations has sheltered an in-bred village lifestyle. Each neighbor here is known through his daily habits; a pattern broken is quickly noticed. A face missing one morning — someone is sure to inqure why. Sticking with what is known: that is the safe feeling. When, all through history, the beloved village is obliterated by earthquake, washed away by flood, the survivors invariably return to rebuild on the very site of their great loss. They are proclaiming their love for the familiar place. When Susie Gentille says, "If I'm gonna die, I'll die with company," and George Moroney recounts how, "When Emma sold me the fish stand, she cried like a baby — the stand was her whole life," they are telling about being comfortable here. It gets in your blood.

Medieval man accommodated to the world, the accident of his birth delineating the fixed form of his future. He accepted his fate and did not seek alternatives. Many children of the Market began life in baskets behind the family stall, the boundaries of their world early defined by the Markethouse. They took up their destiny with an enthusiasm for the personal challenge: the continuation of the family way. When Gordon Wendt tells of forfeiting a four-year college scholarship because his father said, "I need you in the business," and Lucy Roberto Lombardy describes noti-

216

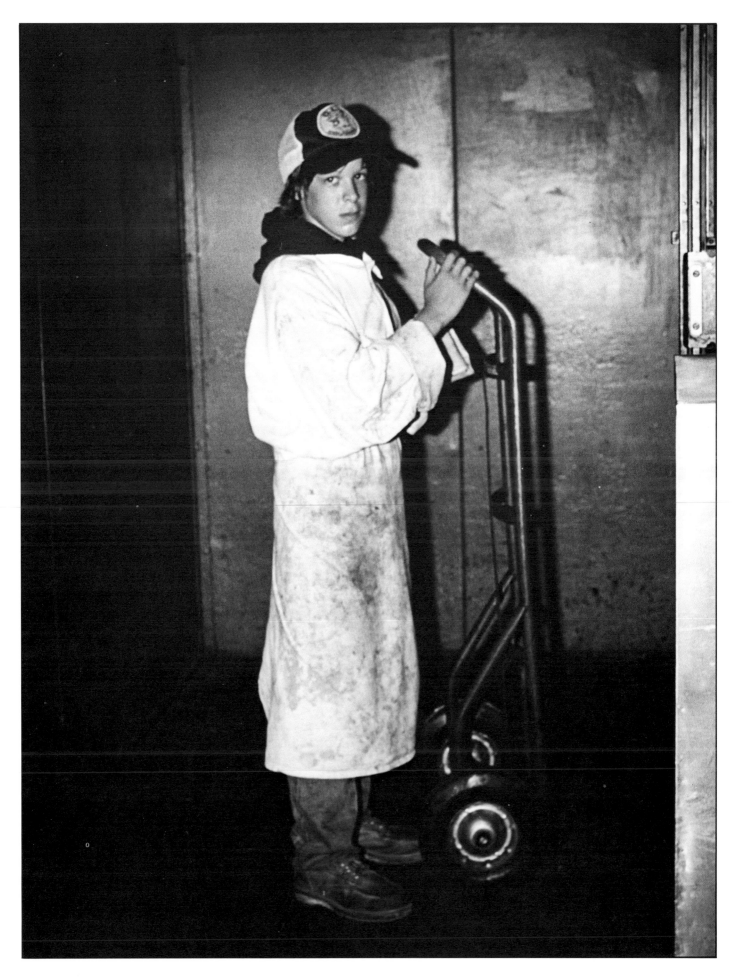

*. . . I have never been much of a shopper, but when I go to the Market, I feel like a pro!

*. . . There has never been a place more rewarding for following your nose!

*. . . I was going around the Market with Steven and I was trying to find a bargain! But, Steven rushed into everything. He bought bologna right off the bat. He asked for two slices, got three slices and paid 20 cents. I asked for two slices of veal bologna, got three slices and the man said I could have them for FREE! So, then Steven started looking for bargains right away. Soon afterwards, we had a real feast.

*VOICES OF CHILDREN, OVERHEARD IN THE MARKET . . .

fying the school authorities that she could not continue, they do not sound bitter. They feel the choice was not theirs to make. It gets in your blood.

The people of the Market seem brave within their harsh work pattern. But don't ask them if they cherish their lives or regret their lives. When Albert Jensch says, "I don't know if I enjoyed my life or not; it was something I grew up in," when Norman Dill says, "Hell, where else am I gonna go?" and when Nate Anselmo's mother, with her dying breath, pleads, "Never leave the West Side Market," they are saying that their expectations for life are different from the popular contemporary dream. Somehow, they don't think that life is so full of the promise and pleasure that many others chase. They prefer to hedge their bets and get THROUGH life rather than take the chance on the unknown. It gets in your blood.

Market life is at once seductive and repulsive! The price one pays for sniffing heavenly dill and sweet melons is the stink of rotten potatoes. The Market can still evoke the past through its sensuality — for our brains are only part of who we are; we need to get a WHIFF of what we forgot. Like the subtle Proustian prodding of memory through sensory stimulus, the remembrance of who we are is tied to mother baking and father sweating and onions browning. With the modern arsenal of deodorizers spraying all the musty odors from our psyches, we are being robbed of our memories! When Robert Stumpf reminisces that it was the "smell of the doggone smoked liver sausage" that lured him back here, and when Edgar Sommer confesses, "I had to get back to where things SPOIL," they remind us that in the Market, unpleasant and uncomfortable make the sweet sweeter. It gets in your blood.

*. . . I wasn't too good at finding the lowest prices, but it was fun talking to the merchants and looking at the, um. . .DIFFERENT kinds of food such as tongue, shark, speared octopus, veal brain and cow head with the EYEBALLS still in it.

*. . . The licorice from the candy stand was great and the dill pickle was delicious.

*VOICES OF CHILDREN, OVERHEARD IN THE MARKET . . .

A man drives all the way from Columbus Ohio, to buy a chunk of Steve Dohar's head cheese; he is craving in that taste a moment somewhere else. Why are such homely delicacies tied to religious holidays and scenes of friendship? The sausage is imbued with spices and is a component of that man's ancestral history; he sinks back into his origins by passionately ingesting that which preceded him. When the Schenck family recounts that no meal was complete without fresh horseradish on the dinner table, they are telling about people who knew that their strength is in their roots! It gets in your blood.

The vendors spend their lives looking out at their fellow man. Sure, a lot of what they see makes them tough, rude, disgusted, tired. But a lot of what they see helps them to recognize a person in need, a person in love, a person who's sick. Animals in the zoo are in danger of losing their prehistoric instincts; the vendors here keep instincts alive through the constant matching of wits, ingenuity, improvisation. How do people get a sense of one another? By taking computerized tests? By watching TV? If you bump up against enough guys, that's how you learn to sniff out what type you're face to face with. To see people in motion, that's the only way to see people. How a person walks, asks a question, handles his money — there is so much to learn here. Rosalie Revay says that even with her back turned, she KNOWS when a customer is coming up to her stand to aggravate her. Jesse Bradley calls this an "intimate place." It gets in your blood.

Public places are depressing today; we don't have access to each other in easy ways. Do people walk their babies in the park? Do couples stroll on the streets after supper? We are afraid of strangers; we lack the PRACTICE of being near one

*. . . From now on, every time I go to the West Side Market with my mom, I can say, "Hey, Mom! I want you to meet Susie Gentille, the Potato Lady!"

another. You can't learn much about the next guy while passing him on the expressway with your windows rolled up and your radio blaring. Why is there the excruciating pain of being close in a crowded elevator? What are we so scared about? We are scared about ourselves, not having the experience of touching. There is fear everywhere — even in our own homes. Yet, here in the Market nobody seems afraid. Maybe it's because in the natural setting of the Market place people feel good, they look good to each other and the activity of the place makes sense to everyone who's here. Mrs. Herman Eggiman doesn't mind traveling the long distance by bus to arrive here because, as she says, "I am EXPECTED at the Market." It gets in your blood.

Can the Market place survive? What will become of this sanctuary, its inviolate tradition tracing back thousands of years through our civilized life? Where will it be, this comfortable space at the center, for giving and taking? WILL IT STAY IN THE BLOOD?

*VOICES OF CHILDREN, OVERHEARD IN THE MARKET . . .